The Character of God

as revealed

in His YHWH Compound Names

Alta Ada Williams

with
Bruce Williams

Lititz Institute Publishing Division

© 2017 by Bruce and Alta Ada Williams

Published by Lititz Institute Publishing Division
P.O. Box 3310, Sequim, WA 98382
www.lititzinstitute.org

All rights reserved. Written permission must be secured from the publisher to use or reproduce any part of this book, except for brief quotations.

Printed in the United States of America

Library of Congress Cataloguing-in-Publication Data

Williams, Alta Ada.
The Character of God as revealed in His YHWH Compound Names / Alta Ada Williams.

    cm.

ISBN 978-0-9820014-8-6   (paperback)

Meaning of Name in the Bible. 2. YHWH Compound Names of God. 3. Applications. I. Title.

All Scripture quotations are taken from The Authorized King James Version of the Holy Bible.

Acknowledgments

In the heavenly realm

Most importantly, I wish to thank the Lord Jesus—Who, although fully God, became fully man, lived a sinless life, and suffered our punishment to reconcile us to God. I thank you that I am God's family.

I also thank the Holy Spirit, Whose inspiration I have sought in writing this book.

In the earthly realm

I give great thanks to Bruce, my husband. We have walked in this spiritual life together and have discussed many of the concepts as God has taught us. I thank him for his encouragement in writing this book, his helpful suggestions, and his love in all things.

I also thank our daughter, Franci Ball, for assistance in proofreading.

Contents

Preface		
1	**Why Study God's Names?**	
2	**Why Study Just The YHWH-Compound Names of God?**	
3	**YHWH Jireh**	יְהוָה יִרְאֶה
4	**YHWH Rapha**	יְהוָה רָפָא
5	**YHWH Nissi**	יְהוָה נֵס
6	**YHWH Shalom**	יְהוָה שָׁלוֹם
7	**YHWH Sabaoth**	יְהוָה צְבָה
8	**YHWH Tsidkenu**	יְהוָׂהוּ צִדְקֵנוּ
9	**YHWH Shammah**	יְהוָה שָׁם
10	**Epilogue**	

Preface

When we consider the character of God, we should always meditate on His power and glory. Isaiah states: "...the whole earth is full of his glory" (6:3b). Thus, we should see God's glory in His creation (the whole earth). The majesty of the Grand Teton National Park illustrates this and shows His glory. The picture on our cover is from that park.

One explanation is necessary concerning a grammatical point. In standard English, pronouns must agree in number and gender with their antecedents. Whenever the gender could be either male or female, standard English uses the male. Thus, the following sentence would be correct: "Each believer must decide for himself what he will do." Since believer is singular and since the gender is not specified, the masculine is used. Modern "politically correct" writers frequently avoid this situation by making the pronoun plural: "Each believer must decide for themselves what they will do." Alternately, some writers use the awkward "Each believer must decide for himself or herself what he or she will do." Neither of these attempts to avoid using the masculine pronoun is acceptable, the former one being incorrect grammar and the latter being very awkward. Thus, in this book we have used the traditional English grammar form, the masculine, when the gender is not specified. Obviously, any statement concerning a believer or an individual should be understood to apply equally to males and females except where context specifically precludes this reading.

All Scriptures are from the Authorized King James Version of The Holy Bible. In the King James Version, when a word is supplied that was not in the original, the translators indicated this fact by putting the word in italics. I have left those in the text; if I add italics, I indicate it.

1
Why Study God's Names?

This chapter will explore the reasons we should study God's names, as revealed in the Scriptures.

As God began to reveal His character to man historically, He used many ways to do this. First, all His acts in history from creation to the end of time serve not only to advance His purposes but also to reveal His character.

As God interacted with man and, more particularly, as He interacted with Israel as a nation, He used His names as a revelation of His character. Names in Hebrew were used to indicate character. Thus, God changed Abram's name (meaning "high father") to Abraham (meaning "father of many nations") to indicate the change in the relationship Abraham had with God. Henceforth, he would be a father of many nations; *i.e.*, he would be fulfilling the covenant promise made by God.

The Hebrew word for *name* is שֵׁם, or *shem*. That is also the name of Noah's son who would carry the seed leading to Messiah. Thus, the name or character is linked to this Son.

The Greek word for *name* is also very interesting. It is ὄνομα, or *onoma*. It derives from another word γινώσκω, or *ginosko*, related to the word meaning "to know." The word had the connotation of understanding in addition. Thus, if one knows someone, he knows his character. The relationship, therefore, between *name* and *character* is maintained in the New Testament. The *Enhanced Strong's Lexicon* states about this word: "[T]he name is used for everything which the name covers, everything the thought or feeling of which is aroused in the mind by mentioning, hearing, remembering, the name."[1]

God changed Jacob's name (meaning "supplanter") to Israel (meaning "God prevails"). This change indicates the progress made by the man who supplanted his brother Esau by purchasing his birthright and stealing the blessing from his father to the man who fathered the children who would become the heads of the twelve tribes of the nation. In fact, the very nation would take its name, Israel, from this new name. And this nation, Israel, would in fact prevail throughout all history. It would be a sign that God and God's plans do prevail.

Having seen that in Hebrew names indicate character, let us look at some implications with respect to the names of God. We will see that all of the promises and actions of God are sealed by His names, indicating His character.

This is one reason for the first commandment—to take God's name in vain is to impugn His character. Exodus 20:7 is one place where this commandment is found: "Thou shalt not take the name of the LORD thy God in vain; for the LORD will not hold him guiltless that taketh his name in vain."

For example, Psalm 91 has some very detailed information concerning God's protection of His people. The promises in this psalm are given to a certain type of person: "Because he hath set his love upon me, therefore will I deliver him: I will set him on high, because he hath known my name" (Psalm 91:14). Thus, the person whom God will deliver is one who has known God's name, or character. That cannot be one without an intimate relationship with God. That relationship is described in verses 1-2 of the same psalm: "He that dwelleth in the secret place of the most High shall abide under the shadow of the Almighty. I will say of the LORD, *He is* my refuge and my fortress: my God; in him will I trust." Verse 14 in more detail is interesting. Hebrew uses parallelism frequently (it says something and then repeats it in another way). It also uses a device called "chiasm." The word derives from the Greek letter χ, or "chi," roughly equivalent to the

English "x." If one imagines the letter "x," with the top left and bottom right ideas parallel and the top right and the bottom left ideas parallel and then reads from left to right, top to bottom, he can understand the chiasm. We have that in verse 14. "Because he hath set his love upon me" is parallel to "because he hath known my name." Knowing God's character and setting our love upon Him cause the other two parts of the chiasm to occur: being delivered and being set on high.

Solomon connects our safety with God's name in Proverbs 18:10: "The name of the LORD *is* a strong tower: the righteous runneth into it, and is safe." Obviously, the righteous does not run into God's name but into the protection provided by God's character.

An even stronger emphasis on God's name occurs when Moses asked to see God's glory. God replied, "I will make all my goodness pass before thee, and I will proclaim the name of the LORD before thee; and will be gracious to whom I will be gracious, and will shew mercy on whom I will shew mercy" (Exodus 33:19). Although Moses was given a glance at only God's back, Moses said, "And the LORD descended in the cloud, and stood with him there, and proclaimed the name of the LORD. And the LORD passed by before him, and proclaimed, The LORD, The LORD God, merciful and gracious, longsuffering, and abundant in goodness and truth" (Exodus 34:5-6). The Lord's showing Moses who He is was linked to His name, indicating His character (merciful and gracious, longsuffering, and abundant in goodness and truth). His name **is** His character.

There are more than 1000 times that the word *name* is used in the Scriptures. Some of those times the word means merely what we usually think when we hear the word: a person or object's name, literally. There are many times, however, when the word is indicating character.

Some examples follow.

In Genesis 2:19 Adam named the animals. Apparently, their names indicated their characteristics.

As mentioned above, Abram's name (as well as Sarai's) was changed to indicated his character (Genesis 17:5, 15).

When Jacob's wives had their children (the names of the future 12 tribes of Israel), they named them for their particular circumstances. For example, when Leah bore her fourth son, "... she conceived again, and bare a son: and she said, Now will I praise the LORD: therefore, she called his name Judah... (Genesis 29:35). The name *Judah* means "praise." It is no accident that it was from this son that the Messiah would come, He to whom all praise is due.

There are scores of other examples showing that names reveal character.

1 Samuel 17: 45 states: "Then said David to the Philistine, Thou comest to me with a sword, and with a spear, and with a shield: but I come to thee in the name of the LORD of hosts, the God of the armies of Israel, whom thou hast defied." Obviously, David did not come in a name, but he came because of the character of God. This Scripture will be examined further in Chapter 7 on יְהוָה צְבָה (the Lord of Hosts).

1 Kings 8:33-34 tells us that when Israel would be disciplined by God, confessing His name is the remedy. Again, this action is not just saying His name; it is acknowledging His character—in this case His righteousness in judging: "When thy people Israel be smitten down before the enemy, because they have sinned against thee, and shall turn again to thee, and confess thy name, and pray, and make supplication unto thee in this house: Then hear thou in heaven, and forgive the sin of thy people Is-

Why Study God's Names? 5

rael, and bring them again unto the land which thou gavest unto their fathers." Confessing God's name mean acknowledging His character.

When God allowed Satan to kill all of Job's children, Job gave a classic response: "Naked came I out of my mother's womb, and naked shall I return thither: the LORD gave, and the LORD hath taken away; blessed be the name of the LORD" (Job 1:21). He recognized that God's character was not impugned by this seeming disaster.

David opens and closes Psalm 8 with these words: "O LORD our Lord, how excellent *is* thy name in all the earth!..."The verses in between describe the works of God that show His character and that He is worthy of this praise. He adds in the following Psalm (vs. 1-2): " I will praise *thee*, O LORD, with my whole heart; I will shew forth all thy marvellous works. I will be glad and rejoice in thee: I will sing praise to thy name, O thou most High." It is not the name as such that David is praising, but the marvelous works mentioned in v. 1—thus, pointing to the character of God. He adds in v. 10: "And they that know thy name will put their trust in thee: for thou, LORD, hast not forsaken them that seek thee." David means that those who know the character of God will put their trust in Him.

One of my favorite verses in this respect is Psalm 20:7, one that I have used many times: "Some *trust* in chariots, and some in horses: but we will remember the name of the LORD our God." In other words, some trust in human or physical solutions, but we will remember the character of God and thus put our trust in Him to deliver us from a difficult situation.

The well-known passage from Isaiah 9:6, predicting the birth of our Lord, shows that His names are linked to His character: "For unto us a child is born, unto us a son is given: and the government shall be upon his shoulder: and his name shall be called Wonderful, Counsellor, The mighty God, The everlasting Father, The Prince of Peace."

The Old Covenant builds the strong case that God's wonderful works enable man to trust Him. This is expressed by the phrase "trust in His name"—*i.e.,* trust His character shown by His works and thus trust Him. The following Scriptures show this facet:

Psalm 29:2 tells us that holiness is the basis for the glory of God's name: "Give unto the LORD the glory due unto his name; worship the LORD in the beauty of holiness." Similarly Psalm 115:1 relates God's attributes as bases to give glory to His name: "Not unto us, O LORD, not unto us, but unto thy name give glory, for thy mercy, *and* for thy truth's sake." Isaiah 57:15 adds to this: "For thus saith the high and lofty One that inhabiteth eternity, whose name *is* Holy; I dwell in the high and holy *place*, with him also *that is* of a contrite and humble spirit, to revive the spirit of the humble, and to revive the heart of the contrite ones."

Psalm 103:1-5 lists many of the character traits that contribute to His name being *holy*: "Bless the LORD, O my soul: and all that is within me, *bless* his holy name. Bless the LORD, O my soul, and forget not all his benefits: Who forgiveth all thine iniquities; who healeth all thy diseases; Who redeemeth thy life from destruction; who crowneth thee with lovingkindness and tender mercies; Who satisfieth thy mouth with good *things; so that* thy youth is renewed like the eagle's."

The New Covenant takes God's name further. Over and over we are told that we can be "saved," or regenerated, by trusting the name of Jesus.

Philippians 2 explains this in detail. Verses 7-8 explain that Jesus "...made himself of no reputation, and took upon him the form of a servant, and was made in the likeness of men: And being found in fashion as a man, he humbled himself, and became obedient unto death, even the death of the cross." Verses 9-10 give the result: "Wherefore God also hath highly exalted him, and given him a name which is above every name: That at the name of Jesus every knee should bow, of *things* in heaven, and *things* in earth, and *things* under the earth." His obedience to the Father caused the Father to exalt Him and give Him a name above every other name. Thus, trusting in His name is trusting in the sacrificial substitutionary atonement that He provided for every man.

The New Covenant numerous times exhorts man to trust in His name. A few examples follow:

Matthew 12:21: "And in his name shall the Gentiles trust."

John 1:12: "But as many as received him, to them gave he power to become the sons of God, *even* to them that believe on his name."

Acts 2:21: "And it shall come to pass, *that* whosoever shall call on the name of the Lord shall be saved."

Acts 4:12: "Neither is there salvation in any other: for there is none other name under heaven given among men, whereby we must be saved."

Romans 10:13: "For whosoever shall call upon the name of the Lord shall be saved."

1 John 3:23: "And this is his commandment, That we should believe on the name of his Son Jesus Christ, and love one another, as he gave us commandment."

In a similar way we are told numerous times that healings and other miracles will occur because of the name of Jesus, *i.e.*, because of His character. Two examples are Mark 16:17-18: "And these signs shall follow them that believe; In my name shall they cast out devils; they shall speak with new tongues; They shall take up serpents; and if they drink any deadly thing, it shall not hurt them; they shall lay hands on the sick, and they shall recover" and James 5:14: "Is any sick among you? let him call for the elders of the church; and let them pray over him, anointing him with oil in the name of the Lord." Peter makes very clear that the miracle of healing is due entirely to appropriating Jesus' name in Act 3:12,16: "And when Peter saw *it*, he answered unto the people, Ye men of Israel, why marvel ye at this? or why look ye so earnestly on us, as though by our own power or holiness we had made this man to walk? And his [Jesus'] sname through faith in his [Jesus'] name hath made this man strong, whom ye see and know: yea, the faith which is by him hath given him this perfect soundness in the presence of you all. "

We are told that the name of Jesus is the most exalted name in the universe: "Far above all principality, and power, and might, and dominion, and every name that is named, not only in this world, but also in that which is to come" (Ephesians 1:21).

One final point concerning Jesus' name is fascinating. In telling us what awaits us in the New Jerusalem, Revelation 22: 4 states: "And they shall see his face; and his name *shall be* in their foreheads." Romans 8:29 tells us that those individuals whom God foreknew would become believers were predestined to be conformed to the image of Jesus: "For whom he did foreknow, he also did predestinate *to be* conformed to the image of his Son, that he might be the firstborn among many brethren." I believe that this Scripture is telling us that when this process is complete, we will be conformed to the image of Jesus. Thus, we will have His character. This is equivalent to having Jesus' name in our foreheads and, therefore, having His character.

Similarly, John tells us: "Beloved, now are we the sons of God, and it doth not yet appear what we shall be: but we know that, when he shall appear, we shall be like him; for we shall see him as he is" (1 John 3:2). Paul makes a similar statement: "The first man *is* of the earth, earthy: the second man *is* the Lord from heaven. As *is* the earthy, such *are* they also that are earthy: and as *is* the heavenly, such *are* they also that are heavenly. And as we have borne the image of the earthy, we shall also bear the image of the heavenly" (1 Corinthians 15:47-49).

This discussion of the use of *name* in the Bible brings us full circle to the question posed at the beginning of the chapter. Why should we study the names of God? Since names indicate character, studying God's names helps us to know God more intimately. As we imprint these names (and God's character) in our spirits, we begin to build up intimacy with God. We build an edifice in our hearts that, in time, brings us closer to being conformed to His image. This study should never be an academic exercise; rather, it should be done in the spirit so that it impacts our very heart.

1. Strong, J. (2001). *Enhanced Strong's Lexicon*. Bellingham, WA: Logos Bible Software.

2
Why Study Just The YHWH-Compound Names of God?

Since there are scores of names of God, we will limit the study for the purpose of this book. The YHWH-compound names of God are ideal for this. They are names of God which have YHWH as part of the name and then are compounded with another name. Taken in the order of their first mention in the Bible, they tell the story of God's redemptive work with man—beginning with God's provision for sinful man to be reunited with God and ending with being in God's presence throughout eternity. There are seven of these names, and seven indicates completion in the Bible. Thus, they give a complete picture of God's work with man.

To understand these names, we must first look at the three primary names of God. The three basic names of God and their first usage in the Scriptures are:

אֱלֹהִים, or Elohim (Genesis 1:1; cp. vs. 26-27)

יְהוָה, or YHWH (Genesis 2:4)

אֲדֹנָי, or Adonai (Genesis 15:2)

We will briefly look at *Elohim* and *Adonai* since this book will concentrate on the YHWH-compound names of God; then we will examine YHWH in more detail.

Elohim is the basic word for God. It is quite interesting. The suffix *–im* is a form for plurality in Hebrew; the Godhead does include plurality. This plurality is indicated in the account of the creation of man: "And God said, Let **us** make man in **our** image, after **our** likeness: and let them have dominion over the fish of the sea, and over the fowl of the air, and over the cattle, and over all the earth, and over every creeping thing that creepeth upon the earth" (Genesis 1:26 [emphasis added]).

Parenthetically, we should note the concept of God in modern Judaism. It uses Deuteronomy 6:4 to insist on monoism in the Godhead rather than plurality or trinity. A close look at the original Hebrew shows this assumption to be false. The verse reads, "Hear, O Israel: The LORD our God *is* one LORD." The word translated "God" is *Elohim*; we have already seen the plural nature of this word. אֶחָד, or *echad*, the word translated "one," actually means many parts gathered into one. Genesis 2:24 gives an example: "Therefore shall a man leave his father and his mother, and shall cleave unto his wife: and they shall be one flesh." Obviously, the "one flesh" is comprised of the man and his wife. A similar use is found in 2 Chronicles 18:12: "And the messenger that went to call Micaiah spake to him, saying, Behold, the words of the prophets *declare* good to the king with one assent; let thy word therefore, I pray thee, be like one of theirs, and speak thou good." The *one assent* was composed of the words of many prophets. There are numerous other examples of this usage of this word, but these serve to show that there was a plurality assumed many times within the word itself. The final word of interest in this verse is יהוה, or YHWH. It is used twice—translated "LORD" both times. Most translations indicate that YWHW is the Hebrew word by using small capital letters (LORD). We will discuss this primary name for God below, but here we will note that it really does not have a number related to it. It indicates existence outside our understanding of grammatical restraints. Thus, it cannot be used to support the idea on monoism in the Godhead.

There are numerous instances where the plurality of the Godhead is clearly indicated in the Old Testament. One such passage is Psalm 110:1: "The LORD said unto my Lord, Sit thou at my

Why Study Just The YHWH-Compound Names of God?

right hand, until I make thine enemies thy footstool." The first *lord* in the verse is YHWH. The second is אֲדֹנִי, or Adonai (also discussed below). This word can be used for one's earthly lord or master as well as for our Heavenly Lord. David was the king of Israel; thus, no one was his earthly lord. So, at the very least, we see two Persons of the Trinity in the verse. Isaiah 48:16 shows the three persons of the Trinity: "Come ye near unto me, hear ye this; I have not spoken in secret from the beginning; from the time that it was, there *am* I: and now the Lord GOD, and his Spirit, hath sent me." God is speaking; thus, He refers to the other two persons of the Trinity. In spite of the concept in today's Judaism, we see that *Elohim* does indicate plurality in the Godhead.

Another of the three primary names of God is *Adonai*. As mentioned above this word can be used for one's earthly lord as well as for our Heavenly Lord. It is first used in Genesis 15:2: "And Abram said, Lord GOD, what wilt thou give me, seeing I go childless, and the steward of my house *is* this Eliezer of Damascus?" The word translated "Lord" is *Adonai*. It is a plural form of a base word meaning "Lord." Since it is coupled with YHWH, which is used only for God, we see that it can be used of our heavenly Lord. Frequently, however, it is used for an earthly lord.

Sarah uses the word to describe Abraham, her earthly lord in Genesis 18:12: "Therefore Sarah laughed within herself, saying, After I am waxed old shall I have pleasure, my lord being old also?"

Another example is its repeated use in the account of Abraham's servant, who was sent to find a bride for Isaac. In Genesis 24:9-64, a singular form of the word, אָדוֹן , or *Adon*, is used 23 times. In each case the servant of Abraham uses it to refer to Abraham, his earthly master. Genesis 24:9 is an example: "And the servant put his hand under the thigh of Abraham his master [*adon*], and sware to him concerning that matter."

Chapter 2

Judaism has once again developed an extra Biblical practice. Since God forbids taking His name in vain, Jewish tradition avoids even using God's redemptive name, YHWH. It substitutes the name *Adonai*. Thus, in reciting Deuteronomy 6:4 (above), known as the *Shema*, taken from the first Hebrew word in the verse, Jewish people recite "Adonai" for each of the two times that YHWH is in the text. *Adonai* is never used in this way in the Bible. Most authorities believe that this substitution was in effect by the second or third century before Christ.

More important to our study is the third primary name of God, YHWH, as we are looking at the YHWH-compound names of God. The word was first used in Genesis 2:4: "These *are* the generations of the heavens and of the earth when they were created, in the day that the LORD God made the earth and the heavens." YHWH is usually written without vowels, as the actual pronunciation is uncertain. This name of God is used, beginning with this verse; but it is not actually explained until Moses' encounter with God in Exodus 3, especially v.14: " And God said unto Moses, I AM THAT I AM: and he said, Thus shalt thou say unto the children of Israel, I AM hath sent me unto you." To understand this word, we must understand something about the Hebrew language. Hebrew is a Semitic language, and Semitic languages are quite different from Indo-European languages (to which group English belongs). Hebrew does not have tense in the same way that the Indo-European languages do. It shows relationships—*i.e.*, event A happened before event B, or event A was a continuous action during which time event B happened. The word translated "I am" is a word that means "existence," without any relation to time. It really indicates just pure existence. This concept supports the Biblical statements that God was and is and is to come, that He is the ever living One. He is outside any force or entity; He is outside all constraints of time. We will see that this meaning is very important in understanding the YHWH compound names of God. This name of God was so powerful that, when Jesus used it at His arrest, the soldiers fell back to the ground: "They answered

Why Study Just The YHWH-Compound Names of God?

him, Jesus of Nazareth. Jesus saith unto them, I am *he*. And Judas also, which betrayed him, stood with them. As soon then as he had said unto them, I am *he*, they went backward, and fell to the ground" (John 18:5–6). The word *he* is not in the original language; Jesus just said, "I am."

This feature of YHWH, that it is outside time constraints, is very important in understanding the compound words. Since this name of God denotes His name throughout all time, it shows that the character trait is one that is eternal. It was not just a name in the Old Covenant; it describes God's character now and forever. Thus, YHWH Tsidkenu, or YHWH our Righteousness, indicates that God is always our righteousness. This is part of his character. This is self evident in most of the names, but it becomes critical in dealing with YHWH Rapha, or God our healer (now and forever).

One last aberration proceeding from Rabbinic Judaism needs to be discussed before studying these compound words. This tradition is also linked to Judaism's avoidance of saying the name of God. As noted above, many times *Adonai* is substituted for YHWH. This practice dates to the second or third century B.C., possibly as far back as the sixth century B.C. Another device was developed over the years to avoid saying God's name. The vowels of YHWH (the Latin "J" is the same as the Hebrew "Y," and the "W" = "V") were combined with the vowels of *Adonai*, thus producing the hybrid *Jehovah*. One reason for this is that the original pronunciation of YHWH was lost, since *Adonai* was substituted at such an early period. Many scholars believe that Yahweh is close, but it is probably better to use the letters YHWH. Most scholars date this tradition in the 12th century A.D., although some would place it in the 5th century. In addition, the vowels are not strictly those of *Adonai*, but they combine some in the word *Elohim*. Some of the early translators of the Bible into English used the word *Jehovah*, but this word has fallen into disuse. Nevertheless, many people are accustomed to using the word with some of the compound names—*i.e., Jehovah Jireh*. We will use the words closer to the Hebrew in this book.

Beginning with God's revelation of this name to Moses, it was associated with His covenant with His people. It is not an accident that He revealed it immediately prior to His delivering His people from bondage in Egypt. As long as His people stayed in their covenant position with God, the blessings associated with each compound name would be theirs.

The seven YHWH-compound names of God and the first mention of each in the Bible follow:

1.
יְהוָה יִרְאֶה

(Gen.22:13-14) YHWH Jireh—the God Who sees (the sacrifice) or Who provides

2.
יְהוָה רָפָא

(Exodus 15:26) YHWH Rapha—the God Who heals

3.
יְהוָה נֵס

(Exodus 17:8-15) YHWH Nissi—the God Who is our banner

4.
יְהוָה שָׁלוֹם

(Judges 6:24) YHWH Shalom—the God Who is our peace

Why Study Just The YHWH-Compound Names of God?

5.

יְהוָה צְבָה

(I Samuel 1:3) YHWH Sabaoth—the Lord of Hosts, or the God Who fights for us

6.

יְהוָה צַדִּיק

(Jeremiah 23:6) YHWH Tsidkenu—the God Who is our righteousness

7.

יְהוָה שָׁם

(Ezekiel 48:35) YHWH Shammah—the God Who is present

Some people identify other YHWH-compound names of God, but none of them is particularly accurate. For example, some people use Psalm 23:1 ("the Lord is my shepherd...") to say that this is a name of God. It is not a name; God is not called "God shepherd." More accurately, this describes a part of God's actions. It would be like saying, "A certain man is a teacher; another man is a doctor."

We will examine the following with each of them—primary meaning, first use in Scripture, others uses in Scripture, fulfillment in Jesus, further applications, and analogy. Some of these will overlap in each name. When we complete the seven, we will see a complete picture of God's dealing with His people (the redeemed down through the ages)—from provision for our redemption (and thus possibility of fellowship with Him) to our spending eternity with Him. In addition, showing that each has fulfillment in Jesus is proof that Jesus is God. The analogy factor probably needs some explanation. To see the picture of God's dealing with His people, we need to see what facet of His dealing that particular name represents. For example, YHWH Jireh shows God seeing a need and responding to that with the solution. Thus, the lamb was provided for Abraham's sacrifice, and the fulfillment in Jesus is that He is pictured as the Lamb of God. Thus the analogy for this name of God is "salvation." And that is the point at which we enter into God's plan. Each of the names will have an analogy in the picture of God's dealing with His people.

We must keep in mind that the use of YHWH (because of its meaning) with each of these names indicates that the particular attribute is eternally God's character. **None of these attributes refers to God solely under the old covenant.** The Gentiles who trust in salvation through Jesus will come out from under the curse and receive the blessing of Abraham ("Christ hath redeemed us from the curse of the law, being made a curse for us: for it is written, Cursed *is* every one that hangeth on a tree: That the blessing of Abraham might come on the Gentiles through Jesus Christ; that we might receive the promise of the Spirit through faith" [Galatians 3:13–14]). Since YHWH is used particularly with God's people who have a relationship with Him, we Gentiles who have believed in Jesus' atoning have access to all these names (and attributes) of God. They represent God's character eternally.

3
YHWH Jireh יְהוָה יִרְאֶה

Primary Meaning

The primary meaning of *YHWH Jireh* is "YHWH looks, sees, provides." As we have learned, YHWH denotes God in a covenantal relationship with His people, Who is outside all time constraints. Thus, He is always looking and seeing man's needs and providing for them. This is His eternal character.

Initial Use

The initial use of YHWH Jireh is found in Genesis 22:14. To understand the use of this name of God, we must study the entire passage of Genesis 22:1-19.

This passage is so important that we will quote it in its entirety:

> [1] And it came to pass after these things, that God did tempt Abraham, and said unto him, Abraham: and he said, Behold, *here* I *am*. [2] And he said, Take now thy son, thine only *son* Isaac, whom thou lovest, and get thee into the land of Moriah; and offer him there for a burnt offering upon one of the mountains which I will tell thee of.
> [3] And Abraham rose up early in the morning, and saddled his ass, and took two of his young men with him, and Isaac his son, and clave the wood for the burnt offering, and rose up, and went unto the place of which God had told him. [4] Then on the third day Abraham lifted up his eyes, and saw the place afar off. [5] And Abraham said unto his young men, Abide ye here with the ass; and I and the lad will go yonder and worship, and come again to you. [6] And Abraham took the wood of the burnt offering, and laid *it* upon Isaac his son; and he took the fire in his hand, and

a knife; and they went both of them together. ⁷ And Isaac spake unto Abraham his father, and said, My father: and he said, Here *am* I, my son. And he said, Behold the fire and the wood: but where *is* the lamb for a burnt offering? ⁸ And Abraham said, My son, God will provide himself a lamb for a burnt offering: so they went both of them together. ⁹ And they came to the place which God had told him of; and Abraham built an altar there, and laid the wood in order, and bound Isaac his son, and laid him on the altar upon the wood. ¹⁰ And Abraham stretched forth his hand, and took the knife to slay his son.

¹¹ And the angel of the LORD called unto him out of heaven, and said, Abraham, Abraham: and he said, Here *am* I. ¹² And he said, Lay not thine hand upon the lad, neither do thou any thing unto him: for now I know that thou fearest God, seeing thou hast not withheld thy son, thine only *son* from me. ¹³ And Abraham lifted up his eyes, and looked, and behold behind *him* a ram caught in a thicket by his horns: and Abraham went and took the ram, and offered him up for a burnt offering in the stead of his son. ¹⁴ And Abraham called the name of that place Jehovahjireh: as it is said *to* this day, In the mount of the LORD it shall be seen.

¹⁵ And the angel of the LORD called unto Abraham out of heaven the second time, ¹⁶ And said, By myself have I sworn, saith the LORD, for because thou hast done this thing, and hast not withheld thy son, thine only *son*: ¹⁷ That in blessing I will bless thee, and in multiplying I will multiply thy seed as the stars of the heaven, and as the sand which *is* upon the sea shore; and thy seed shall possess the gate of his enemies; ¹⁸ And in thy seed shall all the nations of the earth be blessed; because thou hast obeyed my voice. ¹⁹ So Abraham returned unto his young men, and they rose up and went together to Beersheba; and Abraham dwelt at Beersheba.

The word that we transliterate as *jireh*, יִרְאֶה, is composed of two stems. The first letter, the *yodh*, is a shortened form of the word *Jah*, which in turn is a shortened form for YHWH. The rest of the word comes from a stem, רָאָה, or *ra'ah*. It has several meanings. The primary meaning is "to see." It also has the nuances of "look," "consider," "appear," "look after" [by extension "provide"], "regard," and other similar meanings. *Ra'ah* is used four times in the passage from Genesis 22, in addition to giving this name of God, YHWH Jireh—in verses 4 (saw), 8 (provide), 13 (looked), and 14 (seen). The idea behind the word is that God looked, saw that there was need of a sacrifice, and provided for one. Abraham, in turn, saw it. **Looked, saw,** and **provided** are all important parts of this word.

This experience is one of the many in which Abraham exhibited great faith, causing some to call him the father of faith. First, we must understand what God had revealed to Abraham concerning Isaac. God had told Abraham clearly that his seed would come through Isaac: "And God said unto Abraham...in Isaac shall thy seed be called" (Genesis 21:12). Hebrews 11:17-19 tells us how Abraham exercised his faith. God had shown him at some time "in a figure," possibly a dream, that He could raise people from the dead: "By faith Abraham, when he was tried, offered up Isaac: and he that had received the promises offered up his only begotten *son*, Of whom it was said, That in Isaac shall thy seed be called: Accounting that God *was* able to raise *him* up, even from the dead; from whence also he received him in a figure." Abraham's faith was such that he knew that, even if he killed Isaac for the sacrifice, God would raise him from the dead. He knew that God had to do this to keep His promise of the seed's coming through Isaac.

Other Uses in Scripture

The place of the sacrifice, Moriah, is even more interesting. This word is used only twice in the Scriptures, but important events occur there four times. The first time is this instance with Abraham and Isaac. The second occurs in 1 Chronicles 21:1-30 (also 2 Samuel 24). Satan had tempted David to number the children of Israel in disobedience to the Lord. We are told that "...God was displeased with this thing; therefore, he smote Israel" (v. 6). David repented, but God offered him a choice of punishment—three years' famine, three months to be destroyed by enemies, or three days that the sword of the Lord would bring pestilence. David chose the latter, hoping for mercy from the Lord. The Lord saw the destruction and stopped the angel bringing the destruction when he was by the threshing floor of Ornan (or Araunah), a Jebusite. David purchased that land, built an altar at the spot, and sacrificed unto the Lord. Note that verses 15, 16, 20, 21, and 28 have the word *ra'ah*. A similar pattern to that of Abraham shows itself. David needed to sacrifice (for sin), and he did so on this spot. God *saw* the need; David *saw* the angel (instrument of judgment); and David *saw* the Lord's deliverance. Again we see *look*, *see*, and *provide* as integral parts of the episode.

We learn two things in 2 Chronicles 3:1—this place was none other than Mount Moriah and it was the place where Solomon built the temple, the house of the Lord—the third event at that spot ("Then Solomon began to build the house of the LORD at Jerusalem in mount Moriah, where *the LORD* appeared unto David his father, in the place that David had prepared in the threshingfloor of Ornan the Jebusite"). There, for 900 years (with a few disruptions [*e.g.*, 70 years of the Babylonian captivity and after the desecration of the temple at the time of the Macabbees]) sacrifices were made to the Lord. Thus, this place had been established as a place for sacrifice (usually for sins) to YHWH.

It was one of the mountains in the Moriah group on which the Lord Jesus was sacrificed for the sins of the world. Thus, God had established this place as a place of sacrifice, and the supreme sacrifice of all time took place here. What a beautiful picture!

There is even more. First, we must understand that in the Old Testament "**the** angel of the Lord" is the Second Person of the Trinity in His pre-incarnate form. This is shown very clearly in many Scriptures in which the angel of the Lord appears and has some of the characteristics of God, thus being equal with God. The first example of His appearance is to Hagar, after Sarah evicts her from her home. Hagar is by a fountain in the wilderness, is pregnant with Ishmael, and is despairing. The angel of the Lord appears to her and prophesies to her concerning the son she is carrying. After the encounter she names the Lord who spoke to her and the place: "And she called the name of the LORD that spake unto her, Thou God seest me: for she said, Have I also here looked after him that seeth me?" (Genesis 16:13).

Perhaps the most notable appearance of the angel of the Lord is to Moses in the burning bush. Exodus 3: 2-6 relates this encounter: "And the angel of the LORD appeared unto him in a flame of fire out of the midst of a bush: and he looked, and, behold, the bush burned with fire, and the bush *was* not consumed. And Moses said, I will now turn aside, and see this great sight, why the bush is not burnt. And when the LORD saw that he turned aside to see, God called unto him out of the midst of the bush, and said, Moses, Moses. And he said, Here *am* I. And he said, Draw not nigh hither: put off thy shoes from off thy feet, for the place whereon thou standest *is* holy ground. Moreover he said, I *am* the God of thy father, the God of Abraham, the God of Isaac, and the God of Jacob. And Moses hid his face; for he was afraid to look upon God." This passage clearly indicates that the angel of the Lord *is* God. Other examples are the appearance to Balaam in Numbers 22 and the appearance to the parents of Samson in Judges 13. There are many more, but these serve to show that this special angel is none other than the Lord Jesus in His pre-incarnate form. The last appearance of this angel is in Zechariah 12:8. After the incarnation, obviously, Jesus could not appear in this form.

Now, we need to look again at the account of the plague that God sent because of David's numbering of the people. In 2 Samuel 24:16 we see God's decision to stop the plague: "And when the angel stretched out his hand upon Jerusalem to destroy it, the LORD repented him of the evil, and said to the angel that destroyed the people, It is enough: stay now thine hand. And the angel of the LORD was by the threshingplace of Araunah the Jebusite."

We see the very same action as we saw with Abraham on Mount Moriah. Genesis 22:10-12 states: "And Abraham stretched forth his hand, and took the knife to slay his son. And the angel of the LORD called unto him out of heaven, and said, Abraham, Abraham: and he said, Here *am* I. And he said, Lay not thine hand upon the lad, neither do thou any thing unto him: for now I know that thou fearest God, seeing thou hast not withheld thy son, thine only *son* from me [notice that the Angel of the Lord equated himself (me) with God]."

We see the same word used in the passage in Genesis and the one in 2 Samuel for *stretch out*. The Hebrew word is שָׁלַח (*shalach*). This word is in the qal stem; it is usually translated "send," but it is translated "stretch out" or "direct" less often. The picture here is that Abraham (in Genesis 22) and the angel of the Lord (in 2 Samuel 24) stretched out or directed their arms in the sense of sending something. In both cases a sacrifice was involved (Isaac in Genesis and several thousand Israelites in 2 Samuel). God stops both of them and provides another sacrifice—a ram for Abraham and a burnt offering and peace offering for David. What is absolutely breathtaking is that when Jesus was sacrificed for the sins of the world on Mount Moriah, God was unable to stop the hands that performed the killing. He can stop any other sacrifice, but not this one. Jesus had to die for our sins. What love!

Finally, the very name *Moriah* itself is interesting. The "ri" part of the word is the same stem as the one for "see," "provide," and so on. The "ah" is a shortened form for YHWH. Thus, the name itself means "God sees and provides." What does God see? He sees many things, one of which is that all men are in need of a Savior. He tells us in His Word: "... *there is* none that doeth good. The LORD looked down from heaven upon the children of men, to see if there were any that did understand, *and* seek God. They are all gone aside, they are *all* together become filthy: *there is* none that doeth good, no, not one" (Psalm 14:1-3 [also Psalm 53:1-3 and repeated in Romans 3:10-12]). God, therefore, **sees** that men need a Savior, and He **provides** the perfect one in the person of the Lord Jesus. Thus, God's eternal redemptive nature is highlighted in this compound name and even in the place of the first occurrence. We need to note especially Genesis 22:14: "And Abraham called the name of that place Jehovahjireh: as it is said *to* this day, In the mount of the LORD it shall be seen." There is a big play on words in this verse. In giving God's name to this place, Abraham called it YHWH Jireh and said that it would be seen (Jireh) in the **mount** of the Lord. The mount is Moriah, which, as we have seen, contains the stem for the word meaning "God sees or provides." Thus, he was saying that the very name of the mountain embodies this name of YHWH.

Fulfillment in Jesus

As we saw in the previous section, Jesus Himself fulfills this name of God. He is the perfect sacrifice, necessary to take away man's sin. John the Baptist proclaimed this, "The next day John seeth Jesus coming unto him, and saith, Behold the Lamb of God, which taketh away the sin of the world" (John 1:29). The Psalmist (Psalm 14 above), and later Paul (Romans 3:10-12: "As it is written, There is none righteous, no, not one: There is none that understandeth, there is none that seeketh after God. They are all gone out of the way, they are together become unprofitable; there is none that doeth good, no, not one") showed that, when God *looked*, there was not one person who met God's perfect standard. This was not a surprise to God. The preceding paragraph should not be taken to mean that God had to look down to see what to do. God knew and planned for this sacrifice before the foundation of the world: "And all that dwell upon the earth shall worship him, whose names are not written in the book of life of the Lamb slain from the foundation of the world" (Revelation 13:8). Since Jesus became the perfect sacrifice for sin, He is forever known as the Lamb of God. 1 Peter 1:18-19 shows this: "Forasmuch as ye know that ye were not redeemed with corruptible things, *as* silver and gold, from your vain conversation *received* by tradition from your fathers; But with the precious blood of Christ, as of a lamb without blemish and without spot:...."

The book of Revelation, which shows Jesus in His exalted state at the end of the age and into eternity, uses the term 27 times. A few examples follow:

> And I beheld, and, lo, in the midst of the throne and of the four beasts, and in the midst of the elders, stood a Lamb as it had been slain, having seven horns and seven eyes, which are the seven Spirits of God sent forth into all the earth....And when he had taken the book, the four beasts and four *and* twenty elders fell down before the Lamb, having every one of them harps, and golden vials full of odours, which are the prayers of saints.... And I beheld, and I heard the voice of many angels round about the throne and the beasts and the elders: and the number of them was ten thousand times ten thousand, and thousands of thousands; Saying with a loud voice, Worthy is the Lamb that was slain to receive power, and riches, and wisdom, and strength, and honour, and glory, and blessing. And every creature which is in heaven, and on the earth, and under the earth, and such as are in the

sea, and all that are in them, heard I saying, Blessing, and honour, and glory, and power, *be* unto him that sitteth upon the throne, and unto the Lamb for ever and ever.

Revelation 5: 6, 8, 11-13

And they sing the song of Moses the servant of God, and the song of the Lamb, saying, Great and marvellous *are* thy works, Lord God Almighty; just and true *are* thy ways, thou King of saints.

Revelation 15:3

These shall make war with the Lamb, and the Lamb shall overcome them: for he is Lord of lords, and King of kings: and they that are with him *are* called, and chosen, and faithful.

Revelation 17:14

And I saw no temple therein: for the Lord God Almighty and the Lamb are the temple of it. And the city had no need of the sun, neither of the moon, to shine in it: for the glory of God did lighten it, and the Lamb *is* the light thereof.

Revelation 21:22-23

And he shewed me a pure river of water of life, clear as crystal, proceeding out of the throne of God and of the Lamb.... And there shall be no more curse: but the throne of God and of the Lamb shall be in it; and his servants shall serve him:

Revelation 22:1, 3

Chapter 3

Further Applications

There are many applications of this name of God, YHWH Jireh, the God who sees the need and provides the blood sacrifice to fulfill the need. The first instance of the blood sacrifice in Scripture is found in Genesis 3:21: "Unto Adam also and to his wife did the LORD God make coats of skins, and clothed them." Obviously, there was shedding of blood in making the coats of skins. That this act was to show that God required a blood sacrifice to atone for sin is shown by the offerings of the sons of Adam and Eve, Cain and Abel. Genesis 4:3–5a states: "And in process of time it came to pass, that Cain brought of the fruit of the ground an offering unto the LORD. And Abel, he also brought of the firstlings of his flock and of the fat thereof. And the LORD had respect unto Abel and to his offering: But unto Cain and to his offering he had not respect. ..." This pattern held throughout the Old Testament, with the principle stated in Leviticus 17:11: "For the life of the flesh is in the blood: and I have given it to you upon the altar to make an atonement for your souls: for it is the blood that maketh an atonement for the soul." In the tabernacle blood was required for the sin offering and various burnt offerings. Blood was also required when God delivered the Israelites from Egypt. Those who were in houses that had the blood applied to the sides and tops of the doors were "saved" from the Angel of Death .In the New Testament Jesus is called "the Lamb of God" (see above), who provides salvation for us. Jesus Himself said, "I am the way, the truth, and the life: no man cometh unto the Father, but by me" (John 14:6). **God's way of salvation is the only way!**
Jesus emphasized that there is only one way of salvation, through Himself: "Then said Jesus unto them again, Verily, verily, I say unto you, I am the door of the sheep. All that ever came before me are thieves and robbers: but the sheep did not hear them. I am the door: by me if any man enter in, he shall be saved, and shall go in and out, and find pasture" (John 10:7–9).

Peter said to the elders and leaders after he had healed the man on Solomon's porch: "Neither is there salvation in any other: for there is none other name under heaven given among men, whereby we must be saved" (Acts 4:12). John states it very strongly in John 3:16-18: "For God so loved the world, that he gave his only begotten Son, that whosoever believeth in him should not perish, but have everlasting life. For God sent not his Son into the world to condemn the world; but that the world through him might be saved. He that believeth on him is not condemned: but he that believeth not is condemned already, because he hath not believed in the name of the only begotten Son of God" and in John 3:36: "He that believeth on the Son hath everlasting life: and he that believeth not the Son shall not see life; but the wrath of God abideth on him." Paul also stresses this point: "For there is one God, and one mediator between God and men, the man Christ Jesus" (1 Timothy 2:5). Thus, the Apostles Peter, John, and Paul all emphasized that there is only one way of salvation and that is through the Lord Jesus Christ.

Analogy

Thus, the analogy of this name of God is salvation. God looked down from heaven; He saw that there was no righteous man; and He provided the sacrifice necessary. This is indeed part of God's character. We will see many of God's attributes that are shown in His names in Psalm 103:1-5. Verse 3a, in speaking of God, says, "Who forgiveth all thine iniquities."

4
יְהוָה רָפָא YHWH Rapha

Primary Meaning

The second YHWH-compound name of God in order of its appearance in the Bible is *YHWH Rapha*. It indicates that the eternal God is the healer. That is His character and is true for all time and eternity. The word *Rapha* gives us further insight to the meaning of this name. The word itself can mean either "healer" or "physician." In fact, the modern Hebrew word for physician is from the same root. If we look at our circumstances from the spiritual universe, and not the natural one, we would see that God is our physician. We have no need for an earthly one when we appropriate the benefits from the Heavenly one. **[Note: this topic is far too large to be covered adequately in one chapter (just as salvation would be). We will cover a minimum of doctrine to understand the principle. To get a fuller treatment of the subject, read *Healing: What God Has Provided for His Children* (revised edition, 2017), by the same authors.]**

Initial Use

The first use of this name of God is in Exodus 15:26. When the children of Israel came to Marah early in their journey from Egypt to the Promised Land, they could not drink the water because it was bitter; and they murmured against Moses. Moses cried out to God, and God showed him a tree which, when it was cast into the water, caused the water to become sweet. This was a physical illustration of God's healing. He "healed" the waters. This was the time that He revealed this aspect of His character. He said: "... If thou wilt diligently hearken to the voice of the LORD thy God, and wilt do that which is right in his sight, and wilt give ear to his commandments, and keep all his statutes, I will put none of these diseases upon thee, which I have brought upon the Egyptians: for I *am* the LORD that healeth thee." The last phrase of this verse is "YHWH Rapha." *Rapha* is translated "heal," "physician," and other related words in various verses. Thus, just as He "healed" the waters, so God will heal His people who stay in His covenant. For the believer this relates to our following the instructions of the apostle John: "And hereby we do know that we know him, if we keep his commandments. He that saith, I know him, and keepeth not his commandments, is a liar, and the truth is not in him" (1 John 2:3–4). John adds: "And this is love, that we walk after his commandments. This is the commandment, That, as ye have heard from the beginning, ye should walk in it" (2 John 6). Walking in His commandments in the New Covenant is equivalent to keeping God's commandments and statutes in the Old Covenant. That places one in a position from which God can heal him.

Other Uses in Scripture

The Old Testament uses the word *rapha* and related words more than 70 times. Many of these promise complete healing for God's people. Psalm 103 gives one of the clearest statements of God's benefits (including healing). Verses 1-5 state these: "Bless the LORD, O my soul: and all that is within me, *bless* his holy name. Bless the LORD, O my soul, and forget not all his benefits: Who forgiveth **all** thine iniquities; who healeth **all** thy diseases; Who redeemeth thy life from destruction; who crowneth thee with lovingkindness and tender mercies; Who satisfieth thy mouth with good *things; so that* thy youth is renewed like the eagle's" [bold face added]. Just as one of the benefits for God's people is the forgiveness of all sin (iniquities), so is the healing of all diseases. Since this truth has not been taught in many churches, we need to meditate on what the Scriptures say.

Proverbs 4 states a related theme: "My son, attend to my words; incline thine ear unto my sayings. Let them not depart from thine eyes; keep them in the midst of thine heart. For they *are* life unto those that find them, and health to all their flesh" (vs.20–22). The word for *health* comes from the root *rapha*. It means "health, cure, remedy, or healing." An important part of this promise is the intake of God's words and sayings.

This is the same word used when God told Hezekiah through the prophet Isaiah that he would be healed of his mortal illness: "Turn again, and tell Hezekiah the captain of my people, Thus saith the LORD, the God of David thy father, I have heard thy prayer, I have seen thy tears: behold, I will heal thee: on the third day thou shalt go up unto the house of the LORD…..And Hezekiah said unto Isaiah, What *shall be* the sign that the LORD will heal me, and that I shall go up into the house of the LORD the third day?" (2 Kings 20:5, 8).

This word is used frequently in the Old Testament for healing of a people (from their sins). We will discuss later the very close relationship between healing and sin (note this also in the passage from Psalm 103 cited above). Isaiah 6:10 shows this relationship: "Make the heart of this people fat, and make their ears heavy, and shut their eyes; lest they see with their eyes, and hear with their ears, and understand with their heart, and convert, and be healed."

When Hezekiah became king, he was distressed by the people's having turned away from God. He commanded cleansing, and he reinstituted the Passover. It was the greatest Passover since Solomon. As a result, God healed the land: "And the LORD hearkened to Hezekiah, and healed the people" (2 Chronicles 30:20). A similar use of the word is found in 2 Chronicles 7:14. When Solomon had built and dedicated the house of the Lord, the Lord appeared to him in a dream. He gave him some conditions for action if the people strayed from Him in the future. These well-known words are frequently cited by people who want to see their own land "healed," but they were originally given for Israel. There are some valid applications, of course. God said to Solomon: "If my people, which are called by my name, shall humble themselves, and pray, and seek my face, and turn from their wicked ways; then will I hear from heaven, and will forgive their sin, and will heal their land." Approximately one fifth of the uses of *rapha* and related stems refer to healing the land.

These relationships are very significant. The relationship between healing and sin began in the Garden of Eden at the time of the "fall." God had told Adam: "But of the tree of the knowledge of good and evil, thou shalt not eat of it: for in the day that thou eatest thereof thou shalt surely die" (Genesis 2:17). Paul adds: "Wherefore, as by one man sin entered into the world, and death by sin; and so death passed upon all men, for that all have sinned" (Romans 5:12). Thus, by Adam's disobedience sin entered into the world, and death followed that. Illness is, of course, a precursor to death. It is no surprise, therefore, to find healing and sin closely related. This relationship can be taken a step further. At the time that God pronounced a curse, He said, "Because thou hast hearkened unto the voice of thy wife, and hast eaten of the tree, of which I commanded thee, saying, Thou shalt not eat of it: cursed *is* the ground for thy sake; in sorrow shalt thou eat *of* it all the days of thy life; Thorns also and thistles shall it bring forth to thee; and thou shalt eat the herb of the field" (Genesis 3:17–18). Paul tells us more about this curse of the land in Romans 8:19–21: "For the earnest expectation of the creature [creation, lit.] waiteth for the manifestation of the sons of God. For the creature [creation] was made subject to vanity [emptiness, lit.], not willingly, but by reason of him who hath subjected *the same* in hope, Because the creature [creation] itself also shall be delivered from the bondage of corruption into the glorious liberty of the children of God." It is not surprising, then, to see the number of times that the Scriptures speak of God's healing the land. He can heal lands in a temporal way; but the final healing will be when the curse is removed at the end of this age. Paul refers to this in the following verse, verse 22: "For we know that the whole creation [same Greek word translated *creature* above] groaneth and travaileth in pain together until now."

Fulfillment in Jesus

That YHWH Rapha is fulfilled in Jesus is made very clear in the Scriptures. The greatest passage in the Old Testament on Jesus' first advent and death for the sin of mankind is found in Isaiah 53. It is instructive to quote verses 1-11:

> Who hath believed our report? and to whom is the arm of the LORD revealed? For he shall grow up before him as a tender plant, and as a root out of a dry ground: he hath no form nor comeliness; and when we shall see him, *there is* no beauty that we should desire him. He is despised and rejected of men; a man of sorrows, and acquainted with grief: and we hid as it were *our* faces from him; he was despised, and we esteemed him not. Surely he hath borne our griefs, and carried our sorrows: yet we did esteem him stricken, smitten of God, and afflicted. But he *was* wounded for our transgressions, *he was* bruised for our iniquities: the chastisement of our peace *was* upon him; and with his stripes we are healed. All we like sheep have gone astray; we have turned every one to his own way; and the LORD hath laid on him the iniquity of us all. He was oppressed, and he was afflicted, yet he opened not his mouth: he is brought as a lamb to the slaughter, and as a sheep before her shearers is dumb, so he openeth not his mouth. He was taken from prison and from judgment: and who shall declare his generation? for he was cut off out of the land of the living: for the transgression of my people was he stricken. And he made his grave with the wicked, and with the rich in his death; because he had done no violence, neither *was any* deceit in his mouth. Yet it pleased the LORD to bruise him; he hath put *him* to grief: when thou shalt make his soul an offering for sin, he shall see *his* seed, he shall pro-

long *his* days, and the pleasure of the LORD shall prosper in his hand. He shall see of the travail of his soul, *and* shall be satisfied: by his knowledge shall my righteous servant justify many; for he shall bear their iniquities.

There are several important words in this passage. The word translated *grief(s)* in verses 3 and 4 is a word that means "sickness(es)." The word translated *sorrows* means "pain." Another important word is the word translated *borne* in verse 4 and *bear* in verse 11. It is the same word used in Leviticus 16:22 for the scapegoat upon which the sins of the people were put on the Day of Atonement: "And the goat shall bear upon him all their iniquities unto a land not inhabited: and he shall let go the goat in the wilderness." All rules of interpretation state that, if a word has a particular meaning and if the passage does not suggest a change, the word's meaning stays the same. The key word is the one for *bear.* It is obvious in the passage in Leviticus that the goat carried the representation of the sins away, and they were gone. Thus, in Isaiah 53 when verse 11 states that God's servant (whom we will see shortly is Jesus) will bear their iniquities, it refers to the fact that Jesus would bear the sins Himself, and they would be carried away. In verse 4, therefore, when Isaiah says that the servant bore our sicknesses, the same grammatical construction is used. He suffered the sicknesses, and they, too, are gone. There is much more to be gleaned in this passage in Isaiah, but it serves our purposes to point these few things out. The passage shows that healing is available in the atonement.

That Isaiah 53 refers to Jesus is made very clear in the New Testament. Matthew 8:16-17 states that "When the even was come, they brought unto him many that were possessed with devils: and he cast out the spirits with *his* word, and healed all that were sick: That it might be fulfilled which was spoken by Esaias [Isaiah] the prophet, saying, Himself took our infirmities, and bare *our* sicknesses." Peter applies Isaiah 53:5 and 7 to Jesus: "For even hereunto were ye called: because Christ also suffered for us, leaving us an example, that ye should follow his steps: Who did no sin, neither was guile found in his mouth: Who, when he was reviled, reviled not again; when he suffered, he threatened not; but committed *himself* to him that judgeth righteously: Who his own self bare our sins in his own body on the tree, that we, being dead to sins, should live unto righteousness: by whose stripes ye were healed" (1 Peter 2:21–24).

In addition, when Philip was sent to witness to the Ethiopian eunuch, he found the man reading Isaiah 53: 7-8; the eunuch asked of whom Isaiah spoke. We are told that Philip "...opened his mouth, and began at the same scripture, and preached unto him Jesus" (Acts 8:35). Finally, Jesus Himself states that His crucifixion between the thieves (transgressors) was a fulfillment of Isaiah 53:12: "For I say unto you, that this that is written must yet be accomplished in me, And he was reckoned among the transgressors: for the things concerning me have an end" (Luke 22:37).

Since the passages in the Old Testament refer to YHWH as the healer, it is meaningful that Jesus is referred to as the one bringing healing. We see that the Scriptures are very clear that Jesus is the fulfillment of YHWH Rapha. This has many ramifications.

Further Applications

In the Old Testament man was to look upon God as the healer (as revealed in Exodus 15:26. The Scriptures state this many times. Deuteronomy 32:39 is one example: "See now that I, *even* I, *am* he, and *there is* no god with me: I kill, and I make alive; I wound, and I heal: neither *is there any* that can deliver out of my hand." Men were chastised who did not follow God in healing. King Asa is an example of this: "And Asa in the thirty and ninth year of his reign was diseased in his feet, until his disease *was* exceeding *great*: yet in his disease he sought not to the LORD, but to the physicians" (2 Chronicles 16:12). His disease remained until his death. Hezekiah, as seen above, appealed to the Lord, and he was healed.

In the New Testament there are many specific instructions about praying for healing. James 5:14–16 mentions several things to do: "Is any sick among you? let him call for the elders of the church; and let them pray over him, anointing him with oil in the name of the Lord: And the prayer of faith shall save the sick, and the Lord shall raise him up; and if he have committed sins, they shall be forgiven him. Confess *your* faults one to another, and pray one for another, that ye may be healed. The effectual fervent prayer of a righteous man availeth much." The very first thing that James says is for the sick to call for the elders to pray over him and anoint him with oil in the name of the Lord. We should notice that he does not say to go to the doctors. Most people reflexively go to a doctor when they are sick. That is not what the Scriptures tell us to do. In addition, James says that, if we confess our faults to one another and pray for one another, we will be healed since fervent prayer of a righteous man availeth much. (Believers are righteous in the Lord Jesus.)

Jesus specifically said that those who believe would be able to heal people: "And these signs shall follow them that believe; In my name shall they cast out devils; they shall speak with new tongues; They shall take up serpents; and if they drink any deadly thing, it shall not hurt them; they shall lay hands on the sick, and they shall recover" (Mark 16:17–18). Today we are not seeing this mandate of Jesus carried out to a large degree.

The word for *heal* in the New Testament is interesting. Its stem is associated with a word that indicates a healing outside normal processes—suddenly, and sometimes as a sign. We are actually commanded to be healed: "Wherefore lift up the hands which hang down, and the feeble knees; And make straight paths for your feet, lest that which is lame be turned out of the way;

but let it rather be healed"(Hebrews 12:12–13). Every verb in these two verses, including "let it ...be healed," is in the imperative mood. That means that each of them is a command.

As we mentioned earlier, the topic of healing is much too broad to cover in one chapter; but one other aspect needs to be mentioned—that of hindrances to healing. There are many things that can prevent healing. We will mention some without much elaboration; a fuller treatment of them can be found in our book referenced above. Perhaps the two biggest are unbelief (James 1:6; Matthew 17:20-21; Luke 8:48,50; James 5:15) and sin. Jesus states the principle related to unbelief: "Jesus said unto him, If thou canst believe, all things *are* possible to him that believeth" (Mark 9:23). The simplest (and, I suspect, the most frequent) reason why God does not heal is due to sin. There is a direct relationship between sin and death or disease. We discussed the relationship between sin and death or disease above in the section "Other Uses in Scripture."

In Old Testament times God disciplined the Israelites with disease and/or death for their sins. Thus, a fire from the Lord devoured Nadab and Abihu, two of the sons of Aaron, when they offered strange fire before the Lord (Leviticus 10:1-2). The earth opened up and swallowed Korah and his comrades alive who had rebelled against Moses and Aaron, and fire from the Lord consumed the 250 men who offered incense (Numbers 16:1-35). God indicated that some sickness would follow anti-Semitism: "...[the Lord] will lay them [all sickness] upon all those who hate thee" (Deuteronomy 7:15). In Deuteronomy 28:60 sickness is coupled with sin, and David indicates in Psalm 51 that his terrible illnesses and bodily complaints are due directly to his sin.

In the church age God also disciplines us with disease—and occasionally death. Paul writes that many in the Corinthian church were sick and had died (were sleeping) because of unconfessed sin at the communion table (1 Corinthians 11:30). When a believer in the church in Corinth persisted in the sin of incest (1 Corinthians 5:1-5), Paul commanded his body to be turned over to Satan that his soul might be saved. Thus, he was turned over for death because of his sin. In 2 Corinthians 2:4-11, we see that this sentence of death was commuted because he repented. In fact, Paul had to chide the Corinthians because they were so self-righteous that they refused to take him back into fellowship!

When a believer dies because of sin, we say that he has committed the "sin unto death." This terminology comes from 1 John 5:16-17: "If any man see his brother sin a sin which is not unto death, he shall ask, and he shall give him life for them that sin not unto death. There is a sin unto death; I do not say that he shall pray for it. All unrighteousness is sin, and there is a sin not unto death." John indicates that some sins in our lives are such that God decrees our death as a result. He is very clear, however, that not all sin has this sentence of death. John indicates that we can pray for a person who does not commit the sin unto death, and life (opposite of death and its companion, illness) will result. This shows that sin is linked with illness and death. Moses' death was due to sin (Deuteronomy 32:49-52 and 34:7).

Sin, of course, can be mental attitude sins, sins of the tongue, or overt action sins. Because we do not know the heart of a person, we cannot judge whether a person is ill or dies because of sin, apart from revelation from God. God's judgment on sin is almost always different from ours. Isaiah tells us that God's thoughts are higher than ours and that His ways are higher than ours, even to the degree that heaven is higher than the earth (Isaiah 55:9). A list of the seven sins God hates most is in Proverbs 6:16-19. Three are mental attitude; three are sins of the tongue; only murder is an overt action.

On some occasions repentance causes God to annul the death sentence. Two examples of this are King David and the believer in the church at Corinth.

James addresses the "sin unto death," saying that the "prayer of faith shall save the sick, and the Lord shall raise him up; and if he have committed sins, they shall be forgiven him. Confess your faults one to another, and pray one for another, that ye may be healed" (James 5:15-16a). Thus, he implies that if one has not committed sin unto death, confession of sin and prayer will result in healing. We see clearly, therefore, that lack of healing *may* be a result of sin. In its most severe form it is the sin unto death.

There are at least two steps to take before seeking healing. One should confess every known sin, and thus be cleansed from all unrighteousness (1 John 1:9), before seeking healing. Secondly, one should ask the Lord for the "battle plan." (See Chapter 7 "YHWH Sabaoth" for more on this aspect.) When Joshua was leading the children of Israel into various battles to conquer the "Promised Land," he had to ask the Lord the plan for each battle. He did not do this when he tried to conquer Ai. And he suffered defeat (Joshua 7-8). Paul tells us: "Now all these things happened unto them for ensamples [examples]: and they are written for our admonition, upon whom the ends of the world are come" (1 Corinthians 10:11). Thus, we are to ask the Lord for instructions for each "battle" that we face. This includes the battle for healing. Then, and only then, can we declare with David (1 Samuel 17:47), "The battle is the Lord's."

Analogy

The obvious analogy for this name of God for the believer is that God is the Eternal Healer. He will heal us in this life just as He did for the Israelites and as He did when the Lord Jesus was on earth. We just have to believe "in His name" and cleanse our lives in preparation for His work.

5
יְהוָה נִס YHWH Nissi

Primary Meaning

YHWH Nissi literally means "eternal one, banner, ensign, or standard." The Hebrew word נֵס or *nec*, from which *nissi* derives, can mean all of these words. Interestingly enough, it is not always a positive word. Usually it is a standard that God raises to lead His people, but sometimes it indicates a standard raised against people whom He is preparing to judge. We will see that, when the name is fulfilled in Jesus, it has both connotations. Thus, God forever raises His banner to lead His people, but He has also raised up Jesus to judge at the end of the age.

Initial Use

Exodus 17:8-15 contains the initial, and only, use of the complete word *YHWH Nissi* (translated in the KJV as *Jehovahnissi* [review discussion of the origin of the word *Jehovah* at the end of Chapter 2]):

> Then came Amalek, and fought with Israel in Rephidim. And Moses said unto Joshua, Choose us out men, and go out, fight with Amalek: to morrow [sic] I will stand on the top of the hill with the rod of God in mine hand. So Joshua did as Moses had said to him, and fought with Amalek: and Moses, Aaron, and Hur went up to the top of the hill. And it came to pass, when Moses held up his hand, that Israel prevailed: and when he let down his hand, Amalek prevailed. But Moses' hands *were* heavy; and they took a stone, and put *it* under him, and he sat thereon; and Aaron and Hur stayed up his hands, the one on the one side, and the other on the other side; and his hands were steady until the going down of the sun. And Joshua discomfited Amalek and his people with the edge of the

sword. And the LORD said unto Moses, Write this *for* a memorial in a book, and rehearse *it* in the ears of Joshua: for I will utterly put out the remembrance of Amalek from under heaven. And Moses built an altar, and called the name of it Jehovahnissi:

Thus, the initial use indicates that God raised an ensign, in the form of the rod of God, which led His people to victory over their enemies.

Other Uses in Scripture

The word *nec* is used 20 times in the Scriptures. It usually indicates God's raising a standard to lead His people. Psalm 60:4–5 uses the word *nec* to indicate God's deliverance of His people: "Thou hast given a banner to them that fear thee, that it may be displayed because of the truth. Selah. That thy beloved may be delivered; save *with* thy right hand, and hear me." Isaiah adds that His ensign would be raised for the regathering of Israel to her land: "And he shall set up an ensign [*nec*] for the nations, and shall assemble the outcasts of Israel, and gather together the dispersed of Judah from the four corners of the earth" (11:12). Isaiah states similarly in 5:26: "And he will lift up an ensign to the nations from far, and will hiss unto them from the end of the earth: and, behold, they shall come with speed swiftly." Later Isaiah indicates some of the ways that this regathering will occur: "Thus saith the Lord GOD, Behold, I will lift up mine hand to the Gentiles, and set up my standard to the people: and they shall bring thy sons in *their* arms, and thy daughters shall be carried upon *their* shoulders" (49:22) and "Go through, go through the gates; prepare ye the way of the people; cast up, cast up the highway; gather out the stones; lift up a standard for the people. Behold, the LORD hath proclaimed unto the end of the world, Say ye to the daughter of Zion, Behold, thy salvation cometh; behold, his reward *is* with him, and his work before him. And they shall call them, The holy people, The redeemed of the LORD: and thou shalt be called, Sought out, A city not forsaken" (62:10–12). Thus, God's standard will signal both to the nations of the world and to Israel that God is calling His people home (leading them) and that He is redeeming them. In an amazing passage, using a related word, Zechariah in 9:16 states that Israel will actually be an ensign to the land of Israel: "And the LORD their God shall save them in that day as the flock of his people: for they *shall be as* the stones of a crown, lifted up as an ensign [root of *nec*] upon his land."

At this point we need to look at an important principle from Scripture. When there is deliverance/salvation, it is **always** associated with judgment. God's righteousness demands a judgment on evil before He can save or deliver. The first Scripture to promise salvation or deliverance shows this. When Adam and Eve sinned, with Eve's having been enticed by Satan, God first pronounced judgment on Satan: "And the LORD God said unto the serpent, Because thou hast done this, thou *art* cursed above all cattle, and above every beast of the field; upon thy belly shalt thou go, and dust shalt thou eat all the days of thy life: And I will put enmity between thee and the woman, and between thy seed and her seed; it shall bruise thy head, and thou shalt bruise his heel" (Genesis 3:14–15). We should note that Satan would receive a head wound, which is mortal, while effecting a superficial wound (on the heel) of the woman's seed. The apostle Paul makes it clear that the *seed* motif, running throughout the Old Testament, is none other than Jesus: "Now to Abraham and his seed were the promises made. He saith not, And to seeds, as of many; but as of one, And to thy seed, which is Christ" (Galatians 3:16). Paul furthermore tells us about this judgment/saving motif effected by the atoning death of Jesus. Colossians 2:13–15 states: "And you, being dead in your sins and the uncircumcision of your flesh, hath he quickened together with him, having forgiven you all trespasses; Blotting out the handwriting of ordinances that was against us, which was contrary to us, and took it out of the way, nailing it to his cross; *And* having spoiled principalities and powers, he made a shew of them openly, triumphing over them in it." Thus, Jesus "spoiled" the evil powers, openly triumphed over them, and took away the accusations against us due to our sins. He did this so that he could make us alive (quickened us)—*i.e.*, give us the new birth; erase the condemnations; and forgive our trespasses. We see, therefore, judgment associated with deliverance.

We see this same pattern in other deliverances. Peter lists examples of saving and judgment interposed in the events of the flood in Noah's day and the overthrow of Sodom and Gomorrah to state a very important principle: "**The Lord knoweth how to deliver the godly out of temptations, and to reserve the unjust unto the day of judgment to be punished**" (2 Peter 2:9—emphasis added). Other examples are God's judgment on Egypt while saving the children of Israel. The Red Sea's parting was the means of saving the Israelites, but Pharoah's host drowned when the waters closed. This particular salvation/judgment shows another interesting aspect. Saving is always connected with light; judgment, with darkness. For example, the cloud that led the children of Israel to the Red Sea and across it was light to the children of Israel, but it was darkness to the Egyptians. Exodus 14:20 relates this: "And it came between the camp of the Egyptians and the camp of Israel; and it was a cloud and darkness *to them*, but it gave light by night *to these*: so that the one came not near the other all the night." The most prominent example of this concerns the eternal state. On several occasions Jesus describes the place of the demons and unbelievers as one of "outer darkness: there shall be weeping and gnashing of teeth" (Matthew 25:30). This place is also called "the lake of fire": "And whosoever was not found written in the book of life was cast into the lake of fire" (Revelation 20:15). By contrast the eternal abode of the redeemed is a place of light: "And the city had no need of the sun, neither of the moon, to shine in it: for the glory of God did lighten it, and the Lamb *is* the light thereof. And the nations of them which are saved shall walk in the light of it: and the kings of the earth do bring their glory and honour into it. And the gates of it shall not be shut at all by day: for there shall be no night there" (Revelation 21:23–25).

The greatest example of salvation coupled with judgment, of course, is the aforementioned cross of Jesus—condemning sin and the world while providing salvation for all who would believe. We see this pattern with the word *nec* and its corresponding word in the New Testament (see discussion under "Fulfillment in Jesus").

Although *nec* indicates God's leading His people, it is also used as a sign that God is judging people. Usually it is used against people who have gone against God's people, Israel. Thus, the ensign stands for deliverance of God's people but judgment on those opposing Him. We see this in Isaiah 31:9: "And he shall pass over to his strong hold for fear, and his princes shall be afraid of the ensign, saith the LORD, whose fire *is* in Zion, and his furnace in Jerusalem." It can be used in judgment of those in Israel who turn their backs on God, as in Jeremiah 4:3-6: "For thus saith the LORD to the men of Judah and Jerusalem, Break up your fallow ground, and sow not among thorns. Circumcise yourselves to the LORD, and take away the foreskins of your heart, ye men of Judah and inhabitants of Jerusalem: lest my fury come forth like fire, and burn that none can quench *it*, because of the evil of your doings. Declare ye in Judah, and publish in Jerusalem; and say, Blow ye the trumpet in the land: cry, gather together, and say, Assemble yourselves, and let us go into the defenced cities. Set up the standard toward Zion: retire, stay not: for I will bring evil from the north, and a great destruction." Isaiah states a similar idea in 59:19: "So shall they fear the name of the LORD from the west, and his glory from the rising of the sun. When the enemy shall come in like a flood, the Spirit of the LORD shall lift up a standard against him."

God prophesied repeatedly concerning the judgment and destruction of Babylon. He uses a standard to announce this occurrence, as related in Jeremiah 50: 2 and 51:12: Declare ye among the nations, and publish, and set up a standard; publish, *and* conceal not: say, Babylon is taken, Bel is confounded, Merodach is broken in pieces; her idols are confounded, her images are broken in pieces. ... Set up the standard upon the walls of Babylon, make the watch strong, set up the watchmen, prepare the ambushes: for the LORD hath both devised and done that which he spake against the inhabitants of Babylon."

One of the most interesting uses of this word is found in Numbers 21:8-9: "And the LORD said unto Moses, Make thee a fiery serpent, and set it upon a pole [same word—*nec*]: and it shall come to pass, that every one that is bitten, when he looketh upon it, shall live. And Moses made a serpent of brass, and put it upon a pole [*nec*], and it came to pass, that if a serpent had bitten any man, when he beheld the serpent of brass, he lived." This becomes very important in seeing the fulfillment in Jesus, as we will see. Here it indicates God's delivering His people.

Fulfillment in Jesus

The New Testament Greek does not have a word which is an exact parallel with *nec*, but we will see an equivalent. By comparing Numbers 21:8-9 with John 3:14 (discussed under Fulfillment in Jesus), we see that the word ὑψόω (*hupsoo*), which is translated as "lifted up" or "exalted," has much the same meaning and use. It is used 22 times in the New Testament. Most of these uses will be discussed under Fulfillment in Jesus, where they have the most application.

Jesus Himself made the direct connection between this name of God and Himself in John 3:14: "And as Moses lifted up [*hupsoo*] the serpent in the wilderness, even so must the Son of man be lifted up." He repeated this application in John 8:28 and

12:32: "Then said Jesus unto them, When ye have lifted up the Son of man, then shall ye know that I am *he*, and *that* I do nothing of myself; but as my Father hath taught me, I speak these things. ...And I, if I be lifted up from the earth, will draw all *men* unto me."

It was this exaltation of Jesus that allowed Him to be our Savior; thus, He fulfills this name of God, which indicates that God will lift up an ensign to deliver His people. Acts 5:31 indicates this: "Him hath God exalted with his right hand *to be* a Prince and a Saviour, for to give repentance to Israel, and forgiveness of sins." This exaltation also allowed Jesus to send the Holy Spirit, who leads us to victory in our lives in this age: "Therefore being by the right hand of God exalted, and having received of the Father the promise of the Holy Ghost, he hath shed forth this, which ye now see and hear" (Acts 2:33).

We saw that the word *nissi* was used in the Old Testament to indicate times when God raised a banner to show His judgment. We see the same principle with *hupsoo* in the New Testament. Philippians 2:9-11: "Wherefore God also hath highly exalted him, and given him a name which is above every name: That at the name of Jesus every knee should bow, of *things* in heaven, and *things* in earth, and *things* under the earth; And *that* every tongue should confess that Jesus Christ *is* Lord, to the glory of God the Father." Thus, Jesus is exalted, and all people will acknowledge Him to their saving, or they will acknowledge Him in rebellion and under judgment. This passage from Philippians is very interesting in another aspect. God had proclaimed: "Look unto me, and be ye saved, all the ends of the earth: for I *am* God, and *there is* none else. I have sworn by myself, the word is gone out of my mouth *in* righteousness, and shall not return, That unto me every knee shall bow, every tongue shall swear" (Isaiah 45:22–23). The word translated "God" is a shortened form of *Elohim*. The plural ending is omitted. This makes a powerful statement. In Isaiah the Scripture is emphasizing that there is one God and that this obeisance will be to Him. When Philippians states that this will be done to Jesus Christ, it is a strong insistence that Jesus is God. Therefore, this name of God is fulfilled in Jesus.

The Greek word *hupsoo* is used in each of the passages in this section in which the English uses the words *lifted up* and *exalted*. One caveat is that the words *highly exalted* are from a compound word that combines *hupsoo* and a prefix meaning "over," as in "over the top" [*hyper* is a derivative]. The word, then, means "to exalt to the highest rank." Thus, considering Jesus' words in the gospel of John, we see that Jesus is the fulfillment of this name of God.

We also see the opposite side of God's banner that leads His people, that pointing to His judgment, fulfilled in Jesus. Enoch, who was only the seventh man from Adam, saw this aspect very clearly: "And Enoch also ... prophesied of these [men who are condemned—verse 4], saying, Behold, the Lord cometh with ten thousands of his saints, To execute judgment upon all, and to convince all that are ungodly among them of all their ungodly deeds which they have ungodly committed, and of all their hard *speeches* which ungodly sinners have spoken against him" (Jude 14–15).

The apostle John pictures the Lord Jesus coming **down** from the sky to judge the unsaved ones. Thus, men would look up to see Him, as in a banner: "And I saw heaven opened, and behold a white horse; and he that sat upon him *was* called Faithful and True, and in righteousness he doth judge and make war. His eyes *were* as a flame of fire, and on his head *were* many crowns; and he had a name written, that no man knew, but he himself. And he *was* clothed with a vesture dipped in blood: and his name is called The Word of God. And the armies *which were* in heaven followed him upon white horses, clothed in fine linen, white and clean" (Revelation 19:11–14).

Further Applications

Not only is God/Jesus our banner, but He will also lift us up if we come to Him in meekness for deliverance: "Humble yourselves in the sight of the Lord, and he shall lift you up" (James 4: 10) and "Humble yourselves therefore under the mighty hand of God, that he may exalt you in due time" (1 Peter 5:6). We are to "[look] unto Jesus the author and finisher of *our* faith; who for the joy that was set before him endured the cross, despising the shame, and is set down at the right hand of the throne of God" (Hebrews 12:2) in much the same way as the Israelites had to look at the serpent in the wilderness. Jesus said that He would draw all men unto Himself when He was lifted up. We, therefore, look at Him who was lifted up for our salvation; and God, in turn, lifts us up.

We can see another principle of the banner, but using a different word. The *modus operandi* for the travels of the children of Israel was given in Exodus 40:36–38: "And when the cloud was taken up from over the tabernacle, the children of Israel went onward in all their journeys: But if the cloud were not taken up, then they journeyed not till the day that it was taken up. For the cloud of the LORD *was* upon the tabernacle by day, and fire was on it by night, in the sight of all the house of Israel, throughout all their journeys." The word, used three times in this passage and translated "up," comes from a root meaning "ascent" or "upward motion." Thus, just as with *nissi*, the meaning is that they looked for that which was uplifted to guide them. In the last paragraph we saw that we are to look unto Jesus; this is equivalent to the Israelites looking to the cloud. We are told that YHWH was in the cloud: "And the LORD went before them by day in a pillar of a cloud, to lead them the way; and by night in a pillar of fire, to give them light; to go by day and night" (Exodus 13:21). An application for those of us under the New Covenant is to look unto God in the person of the Holy Spirit. When or where the Spirit does not lead, we should not go.

Analogy

This name of God is analogous to our looking to The Exalted One, who is our Savior and who will lead us to victory in our lives. A warning goes with this name. If we do not look to His banner for guidance and leadership, we will see it as judgment against us.

6
יְהוָה שָׁלוֹם YHWH Shalom

Primary Meaning

YHWH Shalom indicates that God forever is peace. Several things flow from this statement, and we will see Scriptures to illustrate them. Jesus is declared to be our Peace; thus He is God, as so many other Scriptures declare. After the cross the only way we can have peace is through Jesus, as we accept His sacrifice for our sins. It is only when our sins are removed that we can have true peace. This peace is not just calmness; it is peace with God. We were at enmity with God until we accepted Jesus as Savior; afterwards we have peace with God. No amount of so-called good works will gain us peace with God.

Initial Use

Judges 6:24 is the first reference to this name of God, YHWH Shalom. The angel of the Lord (Jesus in His preincarnate form) appeared to Gideon and told him that He would deliver his people from the hands of the Midianites. Gideon found this so amazing that he asked the Lord for a sign.

> And he said unto him, If now I have found grace in thy sight, then shew me a sign that thou talkest with me. Depart not hence, I pray thee, until I come unto thee, and bring forth my present, and set *it* before thee. And he said, I will tarry until thou come again. And Gideon went in, and made ready a kid, and unleavened cakes of an ephah of flour: the flesh he put in a basket, and he put the broth in a pot, and brought *it* out unto him under the oak, and presented *it*. And the angel of God said unto him, Take the flesh and the unleavened cakes, and lay *them* upon this rock, and pour out the broth. And he did so. Then the angel of the LORD put forth the end of

the staff that *was* in his hand, and touched the flesh and the unleavened cakes; and there rose up fire out of the rock, and consumed the flesh and the unleavened cakes. Then the angel of the LORD departed out of his sight. And when Gideon perceived that he *was* an angel of the LORD, Gideon said, Alas, O Lord GOD! for because I have seen an angel of the LORD face to face. And the LORD said unto him, Peace *be* unto thee; fear not: thou shalt not die. Then Gideon built an altar there unto the LORD, and called it Jehovahshalom: unto this day it *is* yet in Ophrah of the Abiezrites.

Judges 6:17-24

When Gideon realized that he had talked to the Lord face to face, he was afraid that he would die. God extended peace to him (v. 23) and told him that he would not die. Then Gideon built an altar in that place and called it YHWH Shalom. It is important to note that it is God who extends peace. We cannot have true peace by doing something within ourselves.

Other Uses in Scripture

Many Scriptures indicate that God *is* peace or confers peace other than the one above in Judges. Isaiah tells us in 45:7: "I form the light, and create darkness: I make peace, and create evil: I the LORD [YHWH] do all these *things*." Job indicates much the same thing: "Dominion and fear *are* with him, he maketh peace in his high places" (25:2). Leviticus 26:6 speaks of God's giving peace: "And I will give peace in the land, and ye shall lie down, and none shall make *you* afraid: and I will rid evil beasts out of the land, neither shall the sword go through your land." Numbers 25.12-13 expresses a similar idea. God was rewarding Phinehas for being zealous for God's sake when the children of Israel sinned and gave peace to all his generations: "Wherefore say, Behold, I give unto him my covenant of peace: And he shall have it, and his seed after him, *even* the covenant of an everlasting priesthood; because he was zealous for his God, and made an atonement for the children of Israel."

In the Aaronic blessing God, not the priest, is cited as having to give peace: "The LORD lift up his countenance upon thee, and give thee peace" ("Numbers 6:26). It is important to note that the highest ranking spiritual leader in Israel, the high priest, could not pronounce peace to the people. God only could do that! There are several other Scriptures that say the same thing. Ezekiel (34:25, 37:26) and Haggai (2:9) speak of the peace that God will bring to Israel and Jerusalem once the enmity is destroyed (by the acceptance of Jesus by the remnant). David also tells us that it is God who gives His people peace: "The LORD will give strength unto his people; the LORD will bless his people with peace" (Psalm 29:11). Isaiah makes a similar statement about God's people: "Thou wilt keep *him* in perfect peace, *whose* mind *is* stayed *on thee*: because he trusteth in thee" (26:3). Conversely: "*There is* no peace, saith the LORD, unto the wicked" (Isaiah 48:22).

Fulfillment in Jesus

We need to look at the Scriptures that state that Jesus is also peace. Isaiah gives us the lengthiest list of the names (thus, character) of Jesus in 9:6, and *peace* is one of them: "For unto us a child is born, unto us a son is given: and the government shall be upon his shoulder: and his name shall be called Wonderful, Counsellor, The mighty God, The everlasting Father, The Prince of Peace." Isaiah also adds in the great chapter on the Suffering Servant (Jesus), chapter 53: "But he *was* wounded for our transgressions, *he was* bruised for our iniquities: the chastisement of our peace *was* upon him; and with his stripes we are healed" (vs. 5).

One of the most mysterious passages in the Bible is found in Genesis 14. After Abram and his men defeated Chedorlaomer and the other kings with him and rescued the kings of Sodom and Gomorrah along with his nephew Lot, he met Melchizedek, king of Salem (peace) and priest of El Elyon, the Most high God. Hebrews 7:1-3 amplifies this encounter: "For this Melchisedec, king of Salem, priest of the most high God, who met Abraham returning from the slaughter of the kings, and blessed him; To whom also Abraham gave a tenth part of all; first being by interpretation King of righteousness, and after that also King of Salem, which is, King of peace; Without father, without mother, without descent, having neither beginning of days, nor end of life; but made like unto the Son of God; abideth a priest continually." Many commentators believe that this was an appearance of Jesus in His preincarnate form. The clues for this are the words "without father, without mother, without descent, having neither beginning of days, not end or life, but made like unto the Son of God." Indeed, Hebrews indicates that Jesus' priesthood is after the order of Melchizedek's. Our study on the YHWH names of God gives another clue. In Chapter 8 we will see that Jesus has God's character of righteousness (and, therefore, *is* God); and we are seeing in this chapter that Jesus is also peace. Thus, the writer of Hebrews was indicating Jesus' character by calling this individual the King of righteousness and also the King of peace. Only God (or Jesus, who is God) could be called by these names.

Paul makes it very clear that Jesus is peace: "But now in Christ Jesus ye who sometimes were far off are made nigh by the blood of Christ. For he is our peace, who hath made both [Jew and Gentile] one, and hath broken down the middle wall of partition *between us*" (Ephesians 2:13–14—especially v. 14). We will see that peace in this passage involves this breaking down the partition between Jew and Gentile; and we will see that peace is the result of the breaking down of all other enmities, especially the enmity between God and man. It is the very nature of peace.

Jesus conferred peace on the disciples on several occasions (Luke 24:36; John 14:27, 16:33, 20:19, 20:21, 20:26). Since we have seen that this is something that only God can do, these Scriptures both show that Jesus is God and also show the fulfillment of this name in Jesus.

Further Applications

Another interesting point about God's peace is that He named the individual who would build His house for Him "peace":

> And David said to Solomon, My son, as for me, it was in my mind to build an house unto the name of the LORD my God: But the word of the LORD came to me, saying, Thou hast shed blood abundantly, and hast made great wars: thou shalt not build an house unto my name, because thou hast shed much blood upon the earth in my sight. Behold, a son shall be born to thee, who shall be a man of rest; and I will give him rest from all his enemies round about: for his name shall be Solomon, and I will give peace and quietness unto Israel in his days. He shall build an house for my name; and he shall be my son, and I *will be* his father; and I will establish the throne of his kingdom over Israel for ever.
>
> 1 Chronicles 22:7-10

David reports these words of the Lord, which were given to him before Solomon was born. Because David had been a man of war, he was not allowed to build the house of the Lord. God said that David would have a son who would be a man of peace. He would be "peace." Hebrew does not have vowels in the way English does, and the consonants in Solomon's name are the same as in the word for "peace." Thus, the name *Solomon* means "peace."

Not only did God name the individual who would build His house "peace," but he also named His city ("the city of the great King" [Psalm 48:2, Matthew 5:35]; "the city of our God"

[Psalm 48:1,8]) *peace*. Jerusalem means "teaching of peace." We will see a further application of this aspect of God's name in Chapter 9.

The Bible presents many facets of peace—peace from God, peace with God, peace of God, peace between Jews and Gentiles, and peace on earth.

Peace from God

The account of Gideon at the beginning of this chapter illustrates peace from God, and the examples of God's conferring peace show this as well.

Peace with God

Paul tells us that every man (before the rebirth) is at enmity with God and that, furthermore, this precludes peace [*i.e.*, this is a lack of peace with God]:

> As it is written, There is none righteous, no, not one: There is none that understandeth, there is none that seeketh after God. They are all gone out of the way, they are together become unprofitable; there is none that doeth good, no, not one. Destruction and misery *are* in their ways: **And the way of peace have they not known:** There is no fear of God before their eyes.
>
> Romans 3:10-12, 16-18 (emphasis added)

Paul adds that, when we exercise faith in Jesus' atonement, we have peace with God: "But for us also, to whom it shall be imputed, if we believe on him that raised up Jesus our Lord from the dead; Who was delivered for our offences, and was raised again for our justification. Therefore being justified by faith, we have peace with God through our Lord Jesus Christ" (Romans

4:24–5:1).

Peace of God

The peace of God results only when we are in a saving relationship with Him through Jesus' sacrifice. Philippians 4:7 (see also section on analogy) describes this peace. Exercising faith allows us to experience this peace: "And he said to the woman, Thy faith hath saved thee; go in peace" (Luke 7:50).

When the barrier between God and man is removed, peace results. That barrier can be removed only through faith in Jesus' atoning death on the cross. We see, therefore, that we get peace through Jesus. Interestingly enough, when Peter was presenting Jesus at the house of Cornelius, he said that God had preached peace by Jesus **to the children of Israel**: "The word which *God* sent unto the children of Israel, preaching peace by Jesus Christ: (he is Lord of all:)" (Acts 10:36).

Peace between Jews and Gentiles

We see another barrier that is torn down, resulting in peace, in the relations between Jew and Gentile. Once God chose Israel to be His treasure, His people, mankind was divided into two groups—Jews and Gentiles (all other people groups). In the passage referred to earlier in this chapter, Paul makes this clear:

> That at that time ye [Gentiles] were without Christ, being aliens from the commonwealth of Israel, and strangers from the covenants of promise, having no hope, and without God in the world: But now in Christ Jesus ye who sometimes were far off [Gentiles] are made nigh by the blood of Christ. For he is our peace, who hath made both one, and hath broken down the middle wall of partition *between us*; **Having abolished in his flesh the enmity, *even* the law of commandments *contained* in ordi-**

nances; for to make in himself of twain one new man, *so* making peace; And that he might reconcile both [Jew and Gentile] unto God in one body by the cross, having slain the enmity thereby: And came and preached peace to you which were afar off, and to them that were nigh [Jews]. For through him we both have access by one Spirit unto the Father. Now therefore ye are no more strangers and foreigners, but fellowcitizens with the saints, and of the household of God; And are built upon the foundation of the apostles and prophets, Jesus Christ himself being the chief corner *stone*;

Ephesians 2:12–20 (v. 15 in bold)

Peace on Earth

We have seen that peace results when the enmity between God and man is resolved through Jesus and also when the enmity between Jew and Gentile is resolved (v. 15 above), also through Jesus. Paul, in fact, goes further, **and this is very important.** He says that peace through Jesus' sacrifice will result in peace in all things in the universe. Thus, the nature of peace is the absence of any enmity in the world. Paul says: "And, having made peace through the blood of his cross, by him to reconcile all things unto himself; by him, *I say*, whether *they be* things in earth, or things in heaven" (Colossians 1:20). This peace on earth will not occur until Jesus reigns during the Millennium. Psalm 72:7 describes this time: "In his days shall the righteous flourish; and abundance of peace so long as the moon endureth." The fact that Jesus would bring peace to the universe is foreshadowed by the announcement of the angels at His birth: "Glory to God in the highest, and on earth peace, good will toward men" (Luke 2:14).

Finally, we will note that, since YHWH is peace and since Jesus is peace and since peace is available only through the sacrifice of Jesus, the Godhead—and only the Godhead—can give peace to anyone or anything.

It is very striking that Paul began *every* epistle that he wrote with such words as "grace (or mercy) unto you and peace from God the Father and the Lord Jesus Christ." See Romans 1:7; 1 Corinthians 1:3; 2 Corinthians 1:2; Galatians 1:3; Ephesians 1:2; Philippians 1:2; Colossians 1:2; 1 Thessalonians 1:1; 2 Thessalonians 1:2; 1 Timothy 1:2; 2 Timothy 1:2; Titus 1:4; and Philemon 3. In addition Peter did the same in 1 Peter 1:2 and 2 Peter 1:2. John did the same in 2 John 3, as did Jude in Jude 2. John also makes it clear that this comes from Jesus in Revelation 1: 4: "John to the seven churches which are in Asia: Grace *be* unto you, and peace, from him which is, and which was, and which is to come; and from the seven Spirits which are before his throne." It is significant that the passages in 2 Corinthians, Ephesians, and 2 Peter adjoin verses that have a grammatical construction known as the Granville Sharp rule. When two nouns—both of which being common nouns, personal, and singular—are modified by a single article and are connected by καί, they are always, without exception, referring to the same person. It is important to note in these verses that grace has to come before peace; that is, we cannot have peace unless we have first accepted God's grace in Jesus.

We have seen, therefore, that the Godhead embodies peace. This peace is the absence of any enmity of any kind. God only can give this to His people and that only through the people's acceptance of His provision for tearing down all barriers—the death of Jesus on the cross. YHWH Shalom provides true blessing, that of peace, to the believer. As a member of the Godhead the Holy Spirit can impart this: For the kingdom of God is not meat and drink; but righteousness, and peace, and joy in the Holy Ghost" (Romans 14:17). This verse is key to understanding if we are in proper relationship with God. If we are, we should have peace and joy.

Analogy

The analogy of this name **is** its name—peace. We see two of the facets of this attribute of God in Philippians 4 by comparing verses 7 and 9. Philippians 4:6–9 states: "Be careful for nothing; but in every thing by prayer and supplication with thanksgiving let your requests be made known unto God. And **the peace of God**, which passeth all understanding, shall keep your hearts and minds through Christ Jesus.... Those things, which ye have both learned, and received, and heard, and seen in me, do: and **the God of peace** shall be with you" (emphasis added). Verse 7 refers to the peace of God; that is the peace that God gives to those who have accepted the atoning death of the Lord Jesus. Verse 9 refers to the God of peace; this verse indicates YHWH Shalom—the God Who is Peace.

7
YHWH Sabaoth יְהוָה צְבָה

Primary Meaning

YHWH Sabaoth literally means "Lord of Hosts" or "Lord of Armies." The Hebrew word used is צְבָה or *tsabá*, meaning "host," "war," or "army." The *–oth* indicates plural. Thus, the Lord is eternally (from the meaning of YHWH) identified with the armies. He forever leads the armies of heaven—and the entire universe. This name of God is unique in the number of times it appears. All the other YHWH-compound names of God are used either once or twice, although the characteristic of the name is used many times. This name is used more than 1000 times. We will see the significance of this when we look at further applications.

Initial Use

The first use of this name is found in 1 Samuel 1:3a: "And this man went up out of his city yearly to worship and to sacrifice unto the LORD of hosts in Shiloh...." The account involves Elkanah and his wife Hannah. Hannah was barren, and this was a source of grief to her. Verses 10-11 tell how this name of God was used by Hannah: "And she *was* in bitterness of soul, and prayed unto the LORD, and wept sore. And she vowed a vow, and said, O LORD of hosts, if thou wilt indeed look on the affliction of thine handmaid, and remember me, and not forget thine handmaid, but wilt give unto thine handmaid a man child, then I will give him unto the LORD all the days of his life, and there shall no razor come upon his head."

This was a battle that neither Elkanah nor Hannah could "fight." Thus, Hannah asks the Lord to fight the battle for her, and He did.

Other Uses in Scripture

The other uses in Scripture frequently show that a particular battle is the Lord's to fight. When David fought the giant Goliath, for example, he cried: "Then said David to the Philistine, Thou comest to me with a sword, and with a spear, and with a shield: but I come to thee in the name of the LORD of hosts, the God of the armies of Israel, whom thou hast defied. This day will the LORD deliver thee into mine hand; and I will smite thee, and take thine head from thee; and I will give the carcases [sic] of the host of the Philistines this day unto the fowls of the air, and to the wild beasts of the earth; that all the earth may know that there is a God in Israel. And all this assembly shall know that the LORD saveth not with sword and spear: for the battle *is* the LORD'S, and he will give you into our hands" (1 Samuel 17:45–47). Frequently, the reason for the Lord's fighting the battle is the one David gives in verse 46: "that all the earth may know that there is a God in Israel."

It should be noted that several times God directly states that this is His name. One example is found in Isaiah 47:4: "*As for* our redeemer, the LORD of hosts *is* his name, the Holy One of Israel." Isaiah 48:2 repeats this idea: "For they call themselves of the holy city, and stay themselves upon the God of Israel; The LORD of hosts *is* his name." 2 Samuel 6:2 states the same: "And David arose, and went with all the people that *were* with him from Baale of Judah, to bring up from thence the ark of God, whose name is called by the name of the LORD of hosts that dwelleth *between* the cherubims."

In fact, most of the uses of this name in the Old Covenant state that God is the God of Israel. The name is used in connection with God's covenant relationship with Israel. We will look at several examples, but it is beyond the scope of this book to look at the several hundred relevant passages. The idea, coupling the meaning of this name of God, with His promises to Israel, is that

He will fight the battles for Israel in securing these promises. Jeremiah, particularly, stressed this aspect of the name. He uses the phrase, "the Lord of hosts, the God of Israel," scores of times—literally. Jeremiah uses this name of God, YHWH Sabaoth, an amazing 416 times, and Isaiah uses it 296 times. Almost as amazing is that Zechariah in a much shorter book uses it 225 times. It should be noted that this name of God is used to show that God will fight for Israel; but it is also used when God metes out judgment—both on those people who have come against Israel but also on Israel herself because of her sins against God. Thus, He really is the God of the armies.

After God revealed that He would establish David's house forever, David prayed to that end:

> And now, O LORD God, the word that thou hast spoken concerning thy servant, and concerning his house, establish *it* for ever, and do as thou hast said. **And let thy name be magnified for ever**, saying, The LORD of hosts *is* the God over Israel: and let the house of thy servant David be established before thee. For thou, O LORD of hosts, God of Israel, hast revealed to thy servant, saying, I will build thee an house: therefore hath thy servant found in his heart to pray this prayer unto thee. And now, O Lord GOD, thou *art* that God, and thy words be true, and thou hast promised this goodness unto thy servant: Therefore now let it please thee to bless the house of thy servant, that it may continue for ever before thee: for thou, O Lord GOD, hast spoken *it*: and with thy blessing let the house of thy servant be blessed for ever [emphasis added].
>
> 2 Samuel 7:25–29

Similar to his sentiment in slaying Goliath (testimony before the world), David's sentiment here is that God's name be magnified. That should always be the purpose for God's fighting on our behalf.

There are other significant times when this name is used. When Isaiah saw the Lord in the temple, the seraphim used this name:

> In the year that king Uzziah died I saw also the Lord sitting upon a throne, high and lifted up, and his train filled the temple. Above it stood the seraphims: each one had six wings; with twain he covered his face, and with twain he covered his feet, and with twain he did fly. And one cried unto another, and said, Holy, holy, holy, *is* the LORD of hosts: the whole earth *is* full of his glory. And the posts of the door moved at the voice of him that cried, and the house was filled with smoke. Then said I, Woe *is* me! for I am undone; because I *am* a man of unclean lips, and I dwell in the midst of a people of unclean lips: for mine eyes have seen the King, the LORD of hosts.
>
> Isaiah 6:1–5

This vision of Isaiah's reveals other aspects of the Lord of hosts. He is the king, and the earth is full of his glory. Psalm 24 also stresses these: "Who *is* this King of glory? The LORD strong and mighty, the LORD mighty in battle. Lift up your heads, O ye gates; even lift *them* up, ye everlasting doors; and the King of glory shall come in. Who is this King of glory? The LORD of hosts, he *is* the King of glory. Selah" (vs. 8–10).

Fulfillment in Jesus

The evidence that this name of God is fulfilled in Jesus is more indirect than for some of the other names. One reason for this is that the word *hosts* is not used in the New Testament. We have to compare Scriptures that show this link. One example of that is found by comparing Isaiah 44:6 ("Thus saith the LORD the King of Israel, and his redeemer the LORD of hosts; I *am* the first, and I *am* the last; and beside me *there is* no God.") with the following verses from Revelation:

> I am Alpha and Omega, the beginning and the ending, saith the Lord, which is, and which was, and which is to come, the Almighty.
>
> 1: 8

> Saying, I am Alpha and Omega, the first and the last: and, What thou seest, write in a book, and send *it* unto the seven churches which are in Asia; unto Ephesus, and unto Smyrna, and unto Pergamos, and unto Thyatira, and unto Sardis, and unto Philadelphia, and unto Laodicea.
>
> 1:11

> And he said unto me, It is done. I am Alpha and Omega, the beginning and the end. I will give unto him that is athirst of the fountain of the water of life freely.
>
> 21:6

> I am Alpha and Omega, the beginning and the end, the first and the last.
>
> 22:13

Alpha and *omega* are the first and last letters, respectively, in the Greek alphabet. Thus, Jesus is identifying Himself with the Lord of hosts in Isaiah 44:6. In fact, in this verse in Isaiah the "redeemer the LORD of hosts" probably refers to the second person of the Trinity, since it speaks of **His** (the Father's) redeemer.

We can see another example by comparing verses related to creation. Amos 4:13 explicitly states that the Lord of Hosts is the Creator: "For, lo, he that formeth the mountains, and createth the wind, and declareth unto man what *is* his thought, that maketh the morning darkness, and treadeth upon the high places of the earth, The LORD, The God of hosts, *is* his name." Two passages in the New Testament show that Jesus was the Creator. John 1:1-3 is one of them: "In the beginning was the Word, and the Word was with God, and the Word was God. The same was in the beginning with God. All things were made by him; and without him was not any thing made that was made." Hebrews 1:1–2 states the same: "God, who at sundry times and in divers manners spake in time past unto the fathers by the prophets, Hath in these last days spoken unto us by *his* Son, whom he hath appointed heir of all things, by whom also he made the worlds." Thus, Amos states explicitly that the Creator's name is "the Lord, the God of Hosts." Since John and the author of Hebrews show that Jesus is the Creator, they are saying that Jesus is also the Lord of Hosts.

Another piece of evidence involves Jesus' kingship. Deuteronomy 10:17 states that Yahweh and Elohim are the "Lord of Lords": "For the LORD your God *is* God of gods, and Lord of lords, a great God, a mighty, and a terrible, which regardeth not persons, nor taketh reward." Psalm 136:1 indicates that the Psalmist is referring to Yahweh. In verse 3 he says: "O give thanks to the Lord of lords: for his mercy *endureth* for ever." In Revelation 17:14, the Lord Jesus is given the name *Lord of Lords*: "These shall make war with the Lamb, and the Lamb shall overcome them: for he is Lord of lords, and King of kings: and they that are with him *are* called, and chosen, and faithful." Thus, Jesus is given the name *Lord of Lords*, which was ascribed to Yahweh only in the Old Covenant.

Even though the phrase "Lord of Hosts (armies)" is not used in the New Testament, many Scriptures refer to Jesus as leading the armies of God. Jude mentions that Enoch, the seventh person from Adam, prophesied that Jesus would come to earth with 10,000 saints to judge the unrighteous: "And Enoch also, the seventh from Adam, prophesied of these, saying, Behold, the Lord cometh with ten thousands of his saints, To execute judgment upon all, and to convince all that are ungodly among them of all their ungodly deeds which they have ungodly committed, and of all their hard *speeches* which ungodly sinners have spoken against him" (vs.14-15). This is certainly the same battle as the one mentioned in Revelation 19. Revelation 19:11-13, 16 show that Jesus is the head of the armies of God: "And I saw heaven opened, and behold a white horse; and he that sat upon him *was* called Faithful and True, and in righteousness he doth judge and make war. His eyes *were* as a flame of fire, and on his head *were* many crowns; and he had a name written, that no man knew, but he himself. And he *was* clothed with a vesture dipped in blood: and his name is called The Word of God.... And he hath on *his* vesture and on his thigh a name written, KING OF KINGS, AND LORD OF LORDS." Indeed, Jesus is God and is the fulfillment of His name, *the Lord of Hosts.*

Further Applications

As we have seen, when David battled against Goliath, he stated the principle of God's fighting our battles for us: "Then said David to the Philistine, Thou comest to me with a sword, and with a spear, and with a shield: but I come to thee in the name of the LORD of hosts, the God of the armies of Israel, whom thou hast defied. This day will the LORD deliver thee into mine hand; and I will smite thee, and take thine head from thee; and I will give the carcases of the host of the Philistines this day unto the fowls of the air, and to the wild beasts of the earth; that all the earth may know that there is a God in Israel. And all this assembly shall know that the LORD saveth not with sword and spear: for the battle *is* the LORD'S, and he will give you into our hands" (1 Samuel 17:45–47). God, then, will fight our battles for us in order for the world to know that He is God. The world cannot prevail when God is fighting our battles: "And they shall fight against thee; but they shall not prevail against thee; for I *am* with thee, saith the LORD, to deliver thee" (Jeremiah 1:19). Since God fights our battles, we can say with the apostle Paul: "What shall we then say to these things? If God *be* for us, who *can be* against us?" (Romans 8:31).

We saw earlier that this name of God is used far more than any other. This, in itself, should show us the importance of it. Indeed, a great amount of our walk as believers consists of struggles against the forces of evil (see Analogy). The frequency of the use of this name of God should reassure us that He is always ready to fight our battles if we will let Him.

Analogy

The obvious analogy for the born again person is that he should depend on God to fight his battles. Paul tells us who our enemies are and what we must do in the battle: "For we wrestle not against flesh and blood, but against principalities, against powers, against the rulers of the darkness of this world, against spiritual wickedness in high *places*. Wherefore take unto you the whole armour of God, that ye may be able to withstand in the evil day, and having done all, to stand" (Ephesians 6:12–13). We cannot battle them alone; we must have God's armor and rest in that. Even the archangel Michael did not battle Satan by himself: "Yet Michael the archangel, when contending with the devil he disputed about the body of Moses, durst not bring against him a railing accusation, but said, The Lord rebuke thee" (Jude 9). What a joy to have the God of the universe to fight our battles for us—and he always wins!

8
יְהוָה׀ צִדְקֵנוּ YHWH Tsidkenu

Primary Meaning

YHWH Tsidkenu literally means "Eternal One, Righteousness." Thus, God is eternally the Righteous One.

Initial Use

The initial use of *YHWH Tsidkenu* is found in Jeremiah 23:6: "In his days Judah shall be saved, and Israel shall dwell safely: and this *is* his name whereby he shall be called, THE LORD OUR RIGHTEOUSNESS." The context of this verse is Jeremiah's lamentation about the false and unrighteous shepherds of the people in his day. He prophesies of the day when the people will be regathered into the land, will be saved, and will have a righteous King. Jeremiah says,

> Woe be unto the pastors that destroy and scatter the sheep of my pasture! saith the LORD. Therefore thus saith the LORD God of Israel against the pastors that feed my people; Ye have scattered my flock, and driven them away, and have not visited them: behold, I will visit upon you the evil of your doings, saith the LORD. And I will gather the remnant of my flock out of all countries whither I have driven them, and will bring them again to their folds; and they shall be fruitful and increase. And I will set up shepherds over them which shall feed them: and they shall fear no more, nor be dismayed, neither shall they be lacking, saith the LORD. Behold, the days come, saith the LORD, that I will raise unto David a righteous Branch, and a King shall reign and prosper, and shall execute judgment and justice in the earth. In his days Judah shall be saved, and Israel shall dwell safely: and this *is* his

name whereby he shall be called, THE LORD OUR RIGHTEOUSNESS. Therefore, behold, the days come, saith the LORD, that they shall no more say, The LORD liveth, which brought up the children of Israel out of the land of Egypt; But, The LORD liveth, which brought up and which led the seed of the house of Israel out of the north country, and from all countries whither I had driven them; and they shall dwell in their own land.

Jeremiah 23:1-8

This compound name is found in only one other verse. Jeremiah says: "In those days, and at that time, will I cause the Branch of righteousness to grow up unto David; and he shall execute judgment and righteousness in the land. In those days shall Judah be saved, and Jerusalem shall dwell safely: and this *is the name* wherewith she shall be called, The LORD our righteousness" (33:15-16). These verses are very interesting. Jerusalem is so associated with the Lord Himself that, in discussing the Righteous Branch referred to in Jeremiah 23: 6, Jeremiah uses this name of the Lord to refer to Jerusalem. The picture is that of Israel's being regathered into her land, of her coming to belief in her Messiah, and of her being so linked to these events that she is given one of the Lord's names. This should put a lie to all forms of replacement theology—whether that coming from the organized Church (normally in the Reformed groups) or that coming from the "two-house" adherents. We will discuss this use of the word (for both God and Jerusalem) more in Chapter 10.

The word צִדְקֵנוּ or *righteousness*, comes from צֶדֶק, tsedeq, which is translated as "righteousness" (77 out of 116 times), "just," or "justice." This word comes from a primitive root צָדַק, tsadaq, translated as "justify," "righteous," or "just." These, in turn, are related to צְדָקָה, tsâdaqah, also translated "righteousness" and "justice." To understand the passage in Jeremiah fully, we must look at the extended use of these words in the Old

Testament and of the related word in the New Testament. In addition we need to note that the "branch" is none other than the Lord Jesus. Isaiah and Zechariah make this very clear: "And there shall come forth a rod out of the stem of Jesse [Jesus was descended from Jesse], and a Branch shall grow out of his roots" (Isaiah 11:1). See Zechariah 3:8 and 6:12 for other mentions of this Branch.

Other Uses in Scripture

We will first see that in the Old Covenant the attribute of righteousness was given as an eternal characteristic to God alone—with the caveat of imputation discussed below. In passages such as those above, the name or character trait is also applied to Jesus. In the New Testament we see the same uses of the name.

We must understand the meaning of the words translated "righteousness." We all might have an idea of the meaning of these words, but we must see how God looks at them. For example, we might think of righteousness as a state in which righteous acts are accomplished. See discussion of צֶדֶק, tsedeq above. We might consider certain acts to be good. God, however, does not. He tells us in Isaiah 64:6a: "But we are all as an unclean *thing*, and all our righteousnesses *are* as filthy rags...." Note that it is not our bad acts that are unclean, but our righteousnesses (our so-called good deeds) are filthy. In fact, God also says in Psalms 14:1b-3, "They are corrupt, they have done abominable works, *there is* none that doeth good. The LORD looked down from heaven upon the children of men, to see if there were any that did understand, *and* seek God. They are all gone aside, they are *all* together become filthy: *there is* none that doeth good, no, not one." Paul translates "there is none that doeth good" as "there is none righteous" in Romans 3:10-12.

There are, however, passages in the Scriptures that refer to a righteous man. How do we reconcile these references with the fact that God says that no one is righteous? We get the answer from the first occurrence of one of these words. In Genesis 15: 6 God relates Abram's response to His promises to him: "And he believed in the LORD; and he counted it to him for righteousness." Abram was not righteous in and of himself; but when he trusted the Lord, God imputed righteousness to him. Thus, righteousness is something that we cannot earn by ourselves; God imputes it when we trust in Him. **It is always appropriated by faith.** As we shall see, after the revelation of Jesus as "The Righteous One," that trust involves our acceptance of His substitutionary atonement on the cross for our sins. This is indeed amazing! God actually gives the believer part of His character. All believers will one day be conformed to the image of Christ (Romans 8: 29), but this is the only one of the YHWH-compound names of God that He actually gives to the believer. For example, we never become the one who sees a need and provides (*Jireh*), nor do we become the healer (*Rapha*). Some believers are given the gifts of healing, but we are not the healers—God is the Healer. Similarly, none of the other YHWH-compound names of God is given to us.

The Old Testament portrays righteousness as something eternally resident in God—thus, a part of His character. Psalm 119:142 states: "Thy righteousness is an everlasting righteousness, and thy law is the truth." Note that this Psalm states that this character trait is everlasting, thus agreeing with the concept in the word YHWH. Job also indicates that righteousness is part of God's character: "I will fetch my knowledge from afar, and will ascribe righteousness to my Maker" (36:3). Many other Scriptures ascribe righteousness to God alone and that eternally.

The Psalmist declares: "I will go in the strength of the Lord GOD: I will make mention of thy righteousness, *even* of **thine only**" (Psalm 71:16—emphasis added). God' righteousness is such that, when He swears, He swears by himself: "I have sworn by myself, the word is gone out of my mouth *in* righteousness, and shall not return, That unto me every knee shall bow, every tongue shall swear" (Isaiah 45:23). This Scripture will be important later in showing that Jesus is God. God emphasizes that His righteousness will be forever: "Lift up your eyes to the heavens, and look upon the earth beneath: for the heavens shall vanish away like smoke, and the earth shall wax old like a garment, and they that dwell therein shall die in like manner: but my salvation shall be for ever, and my righteousness shall not be abolished" (Isaiah 51:6). The scope of God's righteousness is infinite: "The LORD *is* righteous in **all** his ways, and holy in all his works" (Psalm 145:17—emphasis added). Finally, at the end of the age God's righteousness is linked to His eternality: "And I heard the angel of the waters say, Thou art righteous, O Lord, which art, and wast, and shalt be, because thou hast judged thus" (Revelation 16:5).

Fulfillment in Jesus

These and other Scriptures, therefore, state that righteousness is an eternal part of God's character and that it is His alone. The Scriptures contain several passages that attribute righteousness to Jesus. This is strong proof, moreover, that Jesus is God. In the passage, quoted above, in which YHWH Tsidkenu is first mentioned (Jeremiah 23:1-8) righteousness is ascribed to the Branch, who is clearly Jesus: "Behold, the days come, saith the LORD, that I will raise unto David a righteous Branch, and a King shall reign and prosper, and shall execute judgment and justice in the earth. In his days Judah shall be saved, and Israel shall dwell safely: and this *is* his name whereby he shall be called, THE LORD OUR RIGHTEOUSNESS" (vs. 5-6). Isaiah 53 contains the fullest account in the Old Testament of Jesus as the suffering servant. Verse 11 ascribes righteousness to Him: "He [the Father] shall see of the travail of his [Jesus'] soul, *and* shall be satisfied: by his knowledge shall my righteous servant justify many; for he shall bear their iniquities."

We saw (above) in Isaiah 45:23 that God's righteousness is the basis for the fact that one day every knee will bow to Him and every tongue shall swear. In Philippians 2: 9-11 we see that this act will be directed toward Jesus; this is strong evidence that Jesus is God: "Wherefore God also hath highly exalted him, and given him a name which is above every name: That at the name of Jesus every knee should bow, of *things* in heaven, and *things* in earth, and *things* under the earth; And *that* every tongue should confess that Jesus Christ *is* Lord, to the glory of God the Father." There are other passages showing that Jesus is righteous in Himself and, therefore, is God. One of these is 1 John 2: 1: "My little children, these things write I unto you, that ye sin not. And if any man sin, we have an advocate with the Father, Jesus Christ the righteous."

There are many, many passages that show that Jesus is the fulfillment of this name of God. 1 Corinthians 1:30 is very clear: "But of him are ye in Christ Jesus, who of God is made unto us wisdom, and righteousness, and sanctification, and redemption." In fact, the identification of this name with David's Righteous Branch (see Jeremiah 23:5 above), who is Jesus, shows very clearly that the fulfillment of this name is found in Him; in fact, He is this name.

Further Applications

We alluded above to the astounding fact that God gives some people this part of His character. How does this happen? It is always appropriated by faith—from Abel to the end of time. Hebrews 11:4 tells us how Abel became righteous: "By faith Abel offered unto God a more excellent sacrifice than Cain, by which he obtained witness that he was righteous, God testifying of his gifts: and by it he being dead yet speaketh." Abel brought to God a blood sacrifice (a foreshadowing of Jesus' later sacrifice) in faith that God would impute righteousness to him. This imputation is made clear over and over in the New Testament. Multiple times we are told that Abraham believed God, and it (his faith) was counted unto (imputed to) him for righteousness—*e.g.*, Romans 4:3, 22; Galatians 3:6; James 2:23.

We should understand that imputation technically does not mean that we have that character trait; it means that God *counts* us as righteous. To understand this fully, we must note that there is a physical universe with which we interact with our physical senses; and there is a spiritual universe which is apprehended with spiritual senses through faith. Paul stresses this principle in 2 Corinthians 4: 18: "While we look not at the things which are seen, but at the things which are not seen: for the things which are seen *are* temporal; but the things which are not seen *are* eternal." In speaking of the creation of things in the natural universe, God says: "Through faith we understand that the worlds were framed by the word of God, so that things which are seen were not made of things which do appear" (Hebrews 11:3).

The great example of one who exercised faith, Abraham, shows a similar principle:

> Therefore *it is* of faith, that *it might be* by grace; to the end the promise might be sure to all the seed; not to that only which is of the law, but to that also which is of the faith of Abraham; who is the father of us all, (As it is written, I have made thee a father of many nations,) before him whom he believed, *even* God, who quickeneth the dead, and calleth those things which be not as though they were. Who against hope believed in hope, that he might become the father of many nations, according to that which was spoken, So shall thy seed be. And being not weak in faith, he considered not his own body now dead, when he was about an hundred years old, neither yet the deadness of Sara's womb: He staggered not at the promise of God through unbelief; but was strong in faith, giving glory to God; And being fully persuaded that, what

he had promised, he was able also to perform. And therefore it was imputed to him for righteousness.

Romans 4:16–22

Thus, when Abraham was fully persuaded (exercise of faith), God imputed the righteousness. At that point of faith, therefore, we are righteous in the spiritual universe.

One of the most important passages on the just (righteous) and on faith is Habakkuk 2:4: "Behold, his soul *which* is lifted up is not upright in him: but the just shall live by his faith." We saw in the discussion of the initial use of *YHWH Tsidkenu* that the word translated "just" is from the same stem as that translated "righteous." This important verse is quoted in three New Testament passages—Romans 1:17, Galatians 3:11, and Hebrews 10:38. All emphasize the necessary component of faith, and the Romans passage relates it to righteousness directly: "For therein is the righteousness of God revealed from faith to faith: as it is written, The just shall live by faith."

It is very important to understand that God imputes righteousness **only** when an individual activates his faith. The following Scriptures show that God is the One who imputes righteousness and/or that this righteousness is obtained through faith:

Psalm 24:5: "He shall receive the blessing from the LORD, and righteousness from the God of his salvation."

Isaiah 54:17: "No weapon that is formed against thee shall prosper; and every tongue *that* shall rise against thee in judgment thou shalt condemn. This *is* the heritage of the servants of the LORD, and their righteousness *is* of me, saith the LORD."

Isaiah 61:10: "I will greatly rejoice in the LORD, my soul shall be joyful in my God; for he hath clothed me with the garments of

salvation, he hath covered me with the robe of righteousness, as a bridegroom decketh *himself* with ornaments, and as a bride adorneth *herself* with her jewels."
Romans 5: 17-19: "For if by one man's offence death reigned by one; much more they which receive abundance of grace and of the gift of righteousness shall reign in life by one, Jesus Christ. Therefore as by the offence of one *judgment came* upon all men to condemnation; even so by the righteousness of one *the free gift came* upon all men unto justification of life. For as by one man's disobedience many were made sinners, so by the obedience of one shall many be made righteous."

Romans 10:10: "For with the heart man believeth unto righteousness; and with the mouth confession is made unto salvation."

2 Corinthians 5:21 (very important): "For he hath made him *to be* sin for us, who knew no sin; that we might be made the righteousness of God in him."

Galatians 5:5: "For we through the Spirit wait for the hope of righteousness by faith."

Philippians 3:9: "And be found in him, not having mine own righteousness, which is of the law, but that which is through the faith of Christ, the righteousness which is of God by faith."

Titus 3:5: "Not by works of righteousness which we have done, but according to his mercy he saved us, by the washing of regeneration, and renewing of the Holy Ghost."

Hebrews 11:7: "By faith Noah, being warned of God of things not seen as yet, moved with fear, prepared an ark to the saving of his house; by the which he condemned the world, and became heir of the righteousness which is by faith."

James 2:23 (similarly Romans 4:3 and Galatians 3:6): "And the scripture was fulfilled which saith, Abraham believed God, and it was imputed unto him for righteousness: and he was called the Friend of God."

1 Peter 2:24 (see more on this verse in Chapter 4): "Who his own self bare our sins in his own body on the tree, that we, being dead to sins, should live unto righteousness: by whose stripes ye were healed."

We saw in Chapter 1 that one purpose of this study is to know God better by knowing His character through His names. This idea is emphasized in the passage above from James. Through exercising faith and having righteousness imputed to us, we have the possibility of being the friend of God. What a blessing and joy!

It is important to note that, although God gives the believer His righteousness, we do not receive the attribute of being able to impute righteousness. Paul clearly states in Romans 3:22–26 that God is the One who can make an individual righteous: "Even the righteousness of God *which is* by faith of Jesus Christ unto all and upon all them that believe: for there is no difference: For all have sinned, and come short of the glory of God; Being justified freely by his grace through the redemption that is in Christ Jesus: Whom God hath set forth *to be* a propitiation through faith in his blood, to declare his righteousness for the remission of sins that are past, through the forbearance of God; **To declare, *I say*, at this time his righteousness: that he might be just, and the justifier of him which believeth in Jesus**" (emphasis added). As noted above, the words *just* and *justifier* have the same stem as the word *righteous*. Receiving this righteousness is part of our being conformed to the image of Messiah. It is part of the substance of God's kingdom: "For the kingdom of God is not meat and drink; but righteousness, and peace, and joy in the Holy Ghost" (Romans 14:17).

What should our response be to this wonderful gift that God bestows upon us? We can do no better than to emulate our father in the faith, Abraham.

> By faith Abraham, when he was called to go out into a place which he should after receive for an inheritance, obeyed; and he went out, not knowing whither he went. By faith he sojourned in the land of promise, as *in* a strange country, dwelling in tabernacles with Isaac and Jacob, the heirs with him of the same promise: **For he looked for a city which hath foundations, whose builder and maker *is* God.** Through faith also Sara herself received strength to conceive seed, and was delivered of a child when she was past age, because she judged him faithful who had promised. Therefore sprang there even of one, and him as good as dead, *so many* as the stars of the sky in multitude, and as the sand which is by the sea shore innumerable. These all died in faith, not having received the promises, but having seen them afar off, and were persuaded of *them*, and embraced *them*, and confessed that they were strangers and pilgrims on the earth. **For they that say such things declare plainly that they seek a country.** And truly, if they had been mindful of that *country* from whence they came out, they might have had opportunity to have returned. **But now they desire a better *country*, that is, an heavenly: wherefore God is not ashamed to be called their God: for he hath prepared for them a city.**
>
> Hebrews 11:8–16 (emphasis added)

We can also look for that city whose builder and maker is God—a better country, a heavenly one—and God will not be ashamed to be called our God.

Chapter 8

Analogy

Thus, this very important YHWH-compound name of God, *YHWH Tsidkenu*, is really the heart of God's plan of redemption of the ages. It is no accident that in order of first use in the Bible it comes second to last, followed by YHWH Shammah, the God who is with us. It is in activating by faith and receiving God's righteousness that we are able to spend eternity with Him.

9
יְהוָה שָׁם YHWH Shammah

Primary Meaning

YHWH Shammah literally means "God [Eternal One—outside of time constraints] Who is present." We will see that this name has far-reaching and exciting applications. It takes us from creation into eternity future.

Initial Use

The only time YHWH Shammah is used in this form is in Ezekiel 48:35: "*It was* round about eighteen thousand *measures*: and the name of the city from *that* day *shall be*, The LORD *is* there." Ezekiel gives this name of God in a passage which is considered by many scholars to describe the Millennial temple, the division of the land between the twelve tribes during that time, and Jesus' reign from Jerusalem. It indicates the presence of the Lord—from that time forward (presumably forever). We will discuss the significance of His name being applied to Jerusalem in the next chapter.

Other Uses in Scripture

Another word, *Immanuel* or *Emmanuel*, has almost the same meaning, "El" (or the Lord) is with us. Isaiah 7:14 states that "… the Lord himself shall give you a sign; Behold, a virgin shall conceive, and bear a son, and shall call his name Immanuel." *Immanuel* is a direct transliteration of the Hebrew words עִמָּנוּ אֵל These *sounds* are carried directly into Greek, where they are used in Matthew 1:23: "Behold, a virgin shall be with child, and shall bring forth a son, and they shall call his name Emmanuel, which being interpreted is, God with us."

Chapter 9

Fulfillment in Jesus

The Scriptures above, showing that one of Jesus' names is *Immanuel/Emmanuel*, indicate that the fulfillment of YHWH Shammah is found in the person of Jesus. Jesus indicated this aspect of His character when He said, "… lo, I am with you alway, *even* unto the end of the world. Amen" (Matthew 28:20b).

This aspect is seen very clearly in an extended passage showing the future New Jerusalem, which will appear as eternity is ushered in:

> And I John saw the holy city, new Jerusalem, coming down from God out of heaven, prepared as a bride adorned for her husband. And I heard a great voice out of heaven saying, Behold, **the tabernacle of God *is* with men, and he will dwell with them, and they shall be his people, and God himself shall be with them**, *and be* their God. And God shall wipe away all tears from their eyes; and there shall be no more death, neither sorrow, nor crying, neither shall there be any more pain: for the former things are passed away. And he that sat upon the throne said, Behold, I make all things new. And he said unto me, Write: for these words are true and faithful. And he said unto me, It is done. I am Alpha and Omega, the beginning and the end. I will give unto him that is athirst of the fountain of the water of life freely. He that overcometh shall inherit all things; and I will be his God, and he shall be my son. But the fearful, and unbelieving, and the abominable, and murderers, and whoremongers, and sorcerers, and idolaters, and all liars, shall have their part in the lake which burneth with fire and brimstone: which is the second death. And there came unto me one of the seven angels which had the seven vials full of the seven last plagues, and talked with me, saying, Come hither, I will shew thee the bride, the Lamb's wife. And he car-

ried me away in the spirit to a great and high mountain, and shewed me that great city, the holy Jerusalem, descending out of heaven from God, Having the glory of God: and her light *was* like unto a stone most precious, even like a jasper stone, clear as crystal; And had a wall great and high, *and* had twelve gates, and at the gates twelve angels, and names written thereon, which are *the names* of the twelve tribes of the children of Israel: On the east three gates; on the north three gates; on the south three gates; and on the west three gates. And the wall of the city had twelve foundations, and in them the names of the twelve apostles of the Lamb. And he that talked with me had a golden reed to measure the city, and the gates thereof, and the wall thereof. And the city lieth foursquare, and the length is as large as the breadth: and he measured the city with the reed, twelve thousand furlongs. The length and the breadth and the height of it are equal. And he measured the wall thereof, an hundred *and* forty *and* four cubits, *according to* the measure of a man, that is, of the angel. And the building of the wall of it was *of* jasper: and the city *was* pure gold, like unto clear glass. And the foundations of the wall of the city *were* garnished with all manner of precious stones. The first foundation *was* jasper; the second, sapphire; the third, a chalcedony; the fourth, an emerald; The fifth, sardonyx; the sixth, sardius; the seventh, chrysolite; the eighth, beryl; the ninth, a topaz; the tenth, a chrysoprasus; the eleventh, a jacinth; the twelfth, an amethyst. And the twelve gates *were* twelve pearls; every several gate was of one pearl: and the street of the city *was* pure gold, as it were transparent glass. **And I saw no temple therein: for the Lord God Almighty and the Lamb are the temple of it**. And the city had no need of the sun, neither of the moon, to shine in it: for the glory of God did lighten it, and the Lamb *is* the light thereof.

Revelation 21:2–23 (emphasis added)

Thus, the Father and the Son make their dwelling with redeemed men throughout eternity, thus fulfilling God's name given in Ezekiel.

There are many Scriptures which point to the fulfillment of this name in Jesus. The apostle John was well aware of what Jesus said about truth, as he records in his gospel in 14:6: "Jesus saith unto him, I am the way, the truth, and the life: no man cometh unto the Father, but by me." Truth, therefore, is a Person, the Lord Jesus. When John says in his second epistle (v.2) "For the truth's sake, which dwelleth in us, and shall be with us for ever," he is stating that Jesus will be with us forever, showing the fulfillment of this name in Him.

Further Applications

There are other exciting applications of this name of God. Paul affirms at the Rapture that "... we which are alive *and* remain shall be caught up together with them in the clouds, to meet the Lord in the air: and so shall we ever be with the Lord" (1 Thessalonians 4:17). Similarly, the passage from Revelation 21, quoted above, states that "the tabernacle of God *is* with men, and he will dwell with them, and they shall be his people, and God himself shall be with them, *and be* their God."

Most of these passages have dealt with eternity, but there are also applications for this life. While we are in this life, moreover, Paul states that God "...hath raised *us* up together, and made *us* sit together in heavenly *places* in Christ Jesus" (Ephesians 2:6). We are with Him in this life.

This is stronger when we consider the work of the Holy Spirit. Paul tells us that "[God] hath also sealed us, and given the earnest of the Spirit in our hearts" (2 Corinthians 1:22). Paul further elaborates on this statement. He tells us (v.7) that we have redemption "that we should be to the praise of his glory, who first trusted in Christ. In whom ye also *trusted*, after that ye heard the word of truth, the gospel of your salvation: in whom also after that ye believed, ye were sealed with that holy Spirit of promise, Which is the earnest of our inheritance until the redemption of the purchased possession, unto the praise of his glory" (Ephesians 1:12–14). The word *earnest* was an old word meaning "down payment," thus indicating the certainty of the transaction. The Holy Spirit comes to dwell with us at the moment of the second birth.

We are told that the bodies of the born again people are the temple of God, as He dwells with us. Paul states in 2 Corinthians 6:16b: "...ye are the temple of the living God; as God hath said, I will dwell in them, and walk in *them*; and I will be their God, and they shall be my people." He adds in Ephesians 2:19-22: "Now therefore ye are no more strangers and foreigners, but fellowcitizens with the saints, and of the household of God; And are built upon the foundation of the apostles and prophets, Jesus Christ himself being the chief corner *stone*; In whom all the building fitly framed together groweth unto an holy temple in the Lord: In whom ye also are builded together for an habitation of God through the Spirit."

When Jesus promised that the Father would send the Holy Spirit, he said that He (the Holy Spirit) would be with us forever: "And I will pray the Father, and he shall give you another Comforter, that he may abide with you for ever; *Even* the Spirit of truth; whom the world cannot receive, because it seeth him not, neither knoweth him: but ye know him; for he dwelleth with you, and shall be in you" (John 14:16–17).

In addition, when God removes us from this life, Paul says that we will be present with the Lord: "Therefore *we are* always confident, knowing that, whilst we are at home in the body, we are absent from the Lord.... We are confident, *I say*, and willing rather to be absent from the body, and to be present with the Lord." (2 Corinthians 5:6, 8). Then, at the culmination of history He will tabernacle with men in the New Jerusalem: "And I saw no temple therein: for the Lord God Almighty and the Lamb are the temple of it" (Revelation 21:22).

We see, then, that not only is God (and Jesus, the Lamb) present with us throughout eternity, but we also have Him present in us (in the person of the Holy Spirit) in this life from the moment of the second birth and forever. We have seen that God/Jesus is present now and throughout eternity. Even more exciting is to see that Jesus has been eternally present with man from eternity past.

The apostle John addresses this point: "In the beginning was the Word, and the Word was with God, and the Word was God. The same was in the beginning with God. **All things were made by him; and without him was not any thing made that was made**" (John 1:1–3—emphasis added). The author of Hebrews goes further: "God, who at sundry times and in divers manners spake in time past unto the fathers by the prophets, Hath in these last days spoken unto us by *his* Son, whom he hath appointed heir of all things, **by whom also he made the worlds**; Who being the brightness of *his* glory, and the express image of his person, and **upholding all things by the word [*rhema*] of his power**, when he had by himself purged our sins, sat down on the right hand of the Majesty on high" (Hebrews 1:1–3—emphasis added). This passage tells us very clearly that Jesus made the worlds, as did John. But this passage goes further. Studying the words in the original Greek for exact meaning and for tense shows that the author is saying that the world is being upheld by Jesus' continual utterances. Thus, He is with us totally in that He is keeping all things operating. So we see that Jesus has been "with us" or with this creation from before creation every single second of time.

Analogy

The analogy of this name of God is the fact that for the one who goes through the second birth God is with him in this life (both by the indwelling Holy Spirit and by his being seated with God in the heavenlies) and that God will be with him throughout eternity. What a marvelous future and hope! In addition, He has been present from eternity past in all of creation.

10
Epilogue

We need to examine the relationship between the YHWH-compound names of God and Jerusalem. We have alluded to this in a small way in some of the preceding chapters. We will also summarize the progressive revelation about Himself that God gives when His YHWH-compound names are studied in the order of their appearance in the Bible.

The Relationship between YHWH and Jerusalem

To understand this relationship, we must look at God's intentions for Jerusalem, stated long before its founding. God gave the following instructions to the children of Israel when they were still in the wilderness under Moses:

> These *are* the statutes and judgments, which ye shall observe to do in the land, which the LORD God of thy fathers giveth thee to possess it, all the days that ye live upon the earth. Ye shall utterly destroy all the places, wherein the nations which ye shall possess served their gods, upon the high mountains, and upon the hills, and under every green tree: And ye shall overthrow their altars, and break their pillars, and burn their groves with fire; and ye shall hew down the graven images of their gods, and destroy the names of them out of that place. Ye shall not do so unto the LORD your God. **But unto the place which the LORD your God shall choose out of all your tribes to put his name there**, *even* unto his habitation shall ye seek, and thither thou shalt come [emphasis added].
>
> Deuteronomy 12:1–5

Deuteronomy 12:11a states that YHWH will have a particular

place where He will put His name: "Then there shall be a place which the LORD your God shall choose to cause his name to dwell there...." Many Scriptures indicate that this would be the case (*e.g.*, Deuteronomy 14:23-24; 16:2,6,17;26:2). God specified the place in 1 Kings 11:36: "And unto his son will I give one tribe, that David my servant may have a light alway before me in Jerusalem, the city which I have chosen me to put my name there." It is mentioned again in this respect in 1 Kings 14:21; 2 Kings 21:4,7; 2 Chronicles 6:6, 12:13, 33:4,7; Nehemiah 1:9; Isaiah 18:7; Jeremiah 3:17, 25:29; and Daniel 9:18-19. We see that there is a relationship between God's name and Jerusalem. It should not surprise us, then, that some of the YHWH-compound names of God are also used for Jerusalem.

We saw in our discussion of God's name, YHWH Jireh, that the very letters in Mount Moriah, the place where Abraham was asked to sacrifice Isaac, embody this name of YHWH. Mount Moriah, of course, is in the heart of Jerusalem.

Jerusalem is actually called by God's name, YHWH Tsidkenu. In Jeremiah 23:6 (quoted in Chapter 8), God Himself is called by that name. That occurs when Jesus, the righteous Branch, sets up a kingdom in Jerusalem, which is conducted in justice and righteousness. Later, in Jeremiah 33:15-16 we are told that this will be the name of Jerusalem herself at that time. We need to note that it is not until there is a righteous kingdom that Jerusalem is called YHWH Tsidkenu (or righteousness). This is fulfillment of God's saying that He would put His name in Jerusalem. He literally will give her His name. How amazing!

A similar pattern—for the same period of time, the earthly kingdom of Messiah during the Millennium—is found with the name YHWH Shammah. Ezekiel tells us: "*It was* round about eighteen thousand *measures*: and the name of the city from *that* day *shall be*, The LORD *is* there" (48:35). Thus, from the time of the Lord's earthly reign and throughout eternity Jerusalem is so identified with YHWH that she receives His name. God had said that He would put His name there. We have seen that *name* in Hebrew indicates character; thus His character is associated with Jerusalem.

There is something more going on than just saying that God's character is associated with Jerusalem. There are many Scriptures which I am convinced we fail to understand because we do not take them literally. The Bible is much more literal than most people realize. When God said in 1 Kings 11:36b that "… Jerusalem [is[] the city which I have chosen me to put my name there," He was being very literal. His name is there—in many of its forms.

God's Revelation about Himself in the YHWH-Compound Names

If we look at the YHWH-compound names of God in the order in which they first appear in the Bible, we see the story of God's relationship with fallen man throughout history and into eternity.

We will briefly show how each name "fits" into the pattern of God's plan of the ages, but one should review that full treatment of each name in the previous chapters to understand this pattern completely.

The first name, *YHWH Jireh*, indicates the "entrance" into God's plan. When Adam fell, sin and death resulted (Romans 5:12—"Wherefore, as by one man sin entered into the world, and death by sin; and so death passed upon all men, for that all have sinned"). There was eternal separation from God. God provided the way of reconciliation. In the Old Covenant the blood sacrifices pointed forward to Jesus' eventual sacrifice. Since the cross the only way of salvation is to trust in His sacrifice. All this is embodied in this name. Jesus Himself said that there is no other way in John 14: 6: "...I am the way, the truth, and the life: no man cometh unto the Father, but by me."

Once we are in God's plan, we can avail ourselves of His healing (*YHWH Rapha*). As we have seen He is forever the Healer. Salvation and healing are linked together in many, many Scriptures (*e.g.*, Psalm 103:2; Isaiah 6:10; John 12:40; Acts 28:27; Exodus 15:26).

As we progress in our life with God, He raises the banner to go before us, guiding us in all our ways (*YHWH Nissi*). This, in turn, gives us peace in all circumstances (*YHWH Shalom*). We are at peace and do not have to fight our battles. He is *YHWH Sabaoth*, the Lord of Hosts; and He fights our battles if we submit to Him.

With further progress we are gradually being changed into the likeness of Him and receive righteousness—both from being in Messiah and from being sanctified in this life (*YHWH Tsidkenu*). During this life God is "with us" (*YHWH Shammah*) in the form of the indwelling Holy Spirit. Finally, at the end of this earthly existence we will forever be with the Lord: "...and so shall we ever be with the Lord" (1 Thessalonians 4:17b).

By understanding the YHWH-compound names of God (and thus His character)—not an intellectual knowledge, but an understanding that is deeply embedded into our spirits—we can more fully live the life God has prepared for us. We will know Him more and will draw very close to Him. We will also have victory in our walk with Him. What an exciting life we can live!

www.ingramcontent.com/pod-product-compliance
Lightning Source LLC
Chambersburg PA
CBHW050915160426
43194CB00011B/2413